Haunted Encounters

Ghost Stories from Around the World

Edited by Ginnie Siena Bivona, Mitchel Whitington, and Dorothy McConachie

Atriad Press • Dallas, Texas

Editors

Inquiries should be addressed to

Atriad Press
13820 Methuen Green
Dallas Texas, 75240
972-671-0002
AtriadPress.com

Library of Congress Control Number 2004103231

ISBN 0-9740394-1-1

The editors wish to thank Alan McCuller for the outstanding cover art,
Martha McCuller for the beautiful interior design,
and Beth Kohler and Faye Voorhis for their excellent editorial work.
We are very grateful for their contributions.

1 3 5 7 9 8 6 4 2
Printed in the United States of America

Publishers do not exist except for writers, just as writers cannot live without readers. This book is dedicated to both; the tireless writer, tweaking, adjusting, striving endlessly to paint a picture in words, and the fascinated reader, taking the words into their mind and seeing the picture complete. We all touch one another in the most amazing way, from mind to mind, around the planet, through the exquisite magic of the book. As publishers we are extraordinarily grateful for all of you.

Look for other titles from the Haunted Encounters series:

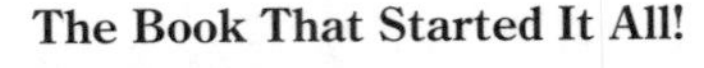
The Book That Started It All!

Haunted Encounters: Real-Life Stories of Supernatural Experiences

Real Stories. Real people. Real haunted encounters. Delve into authentic tales of the supernatural, as told by the people who lived them. Forty-six stories of the unknown; some will touch you, others will make you smile, and many will make you want to sleep with the lights on. In bookstores everywhere.

ISBN 0-9740394-0-3

The Most Unique Book of True Ghost Stories You've Ever Read!

Haunted Encounters: Personal Stories of Departed Pets

The deep bond between animals and humans has never been so well demonstrated as in the pages of these true accounts of ghostly encounters with beloved pets. Curl up with your favorite furry friends and enjoy this loving collection of interesting experiences by real people.

ISBN 0-9740394-2-X

Meet the Spirits of Departed Family & Friends

Haunted Encounters: Departed Family & Friends

Perhaps the most touching form of ghostly encounters is that with a family member or friend who's passed on. This book features true ghost stories of such events — you'll laugh with one author while crying with another. Above all, you will discover that losing a loved one doesn't necessarily mean that they're gone.

Available Fall 2004
ISBN 0-9740394-3-8

A World-Famous Ghost Hunter Speaks

Fear: A Ghost Hunter's Story

What do you get when one of the world's foremost ghost hunters and veteran of supernatural television shows (including MTV's *Fear*) puts pen to paper to tell her story? You get one of the most interesting books on the spirit world that you're likely to find. Join Kriss on her many adventures, and learn about her innermost thoughts on the supernatural.

Available Fall 2004
ISBN 0-9740394-4-6

Pack Your Bags for a Spirited Trip

A Ghost in My Suitcase:
A Guide to Haunted Travel in America

Mitchel Whitington has traveled the country looking for some of the most haunted destinations, and tells the stories in his latest book. You may have heard him speak at conferences, or on radio programs, but now you have a chance to accompany him in search of the most interesting haunted places in America.

Available Fall 2004
ISBN 0-9740394-5-4

For ordering information

www.atriadpress.com

Atriad Press
13820 Methuen Green
Dallas, TX 75240
972-671-0002

Contents

Introduction

When I was young, on those rare occasions when an airplane flew over our house everyone ran outside to see. Phones had short cords, and the coal for our furnace came in a horse drawn wagon. I'll admit, I'm not a kid anymore, but I am not that old either.

Still, the way the world is today astounds me. Anything, anyone, any place, and even any time period is right here in front of me on a little white screen. Key it in, and there it is. Whatever that "it" is that you are seeking.

When we started planning for the *Haunted Encounters* series, we knew that the best way to introduce our books to the writers across the U.S. was by simply contacting some on-line writers groups, and pretty quickly, we figured, we'd have plenty of submissions. What we didn't expect was the number of stories flooding in from all over the world! The word spread across oceans and continents, from country to country, around the planet.

From Dallas to New Delhi, from Italy and Ireland, England, Scotland and Canada. It still takes two days to fly to Australia, but I can get there in seconds. New Zealand is nine pecks at my keyboard. The Philippines, and far off Japan. Not far off anymore.

Even more beautiful, we are not doing business with dry pieces of paper, stories written, sent in and forgotten about. We are doing business with people... real live human beings we can talk to, learn a little about, become friends. E-mails flash back and forth across a million miles. We visit, wish each other well, encourage one another.

Suddenly we are not just publishers. Laid out on these pages are the experiences our friends have had, amazing, sometimes scary, sometimes wonderful, and always personal.

So, it gives us great pleasure to bring you this new collection of *Haunted Encounters.* We love these stories, and we know you will too.

Ginnie Siena Bivona
President, Atriad Press
April, 2004

The Silent Man

by Angela Vale
London, England

It was curious, the feeling I had of recognition as soon as I saw the house. It was not so much that it was just what we'd been looking for, but a certainty that it belonged to us. It had always belonged to us. That was why we'd worked so hard to find it.

At the time we were living along the coast from Dun Laoghaire, the town about eight miles from Dublin where the boat comes in, bringing hordes of summer visitors.

We knew we'd outgrown our much-loved cottage when our third daughter, Katie, was born, although we managed fairly well for two more years, until we realized that it was either the growing army of Katie's soft toys or us. There simply wasn't room for both. But it was more than the need for space that made us so desperate to find another house. Although we didn't recognize it at the time, it was our house calling to us.

As I pulled myself up on the high, rusted iron gate in an attempt to see more clearly, I felt I'd come home. And in spite of the pain of fighting my way with sandaled feet through the vicious brambles and nettles that twisted their way the length of the overgrown garden, I knew that whatever happened, I had to get inside. Then I felt a sudden wave of panic.

Suppose if, after all these years of neglect, the house had been spotted by someone else. Suppose even now that someone was signing on the dotted line. For months the estate agent had been sending us details of unsuitable properties; mostly modern and surrounded by rows of similar houses.

"But we're looking for somewhere on its own, somewhere with a bit of character," I'd hear myself bleating for what felt like the hundredth time. Why couldn't the wretched man understand? He had an annoying habit of tipping his head to one side, and giving me a roguish wink, as if to say, "Trust me. I know what's best for you." And now here I was, at the end of a leafy lane, where the only sounds were a distant lawnmower, the old push-type, and a solitary bird serenading the fitful sun.

"No one's been to see this one for months." The winking estate agent had pushed details of the house across his desk to me that morning, following it with a bunch of keys. "Might be what you're looking for. Easy enough to find. Straight up the hill from the sea-front gardens." He turned away and started taking papers out of a filing cabinet. Plainly he'd lost interest in us and our quest for "something different."

"If this one isn't right, then… anyway, there's a kind of a lane, trees and bushes leading off the main road. Go along it for a few yards, turn a corner, and right in front of you… it's the first of four old houses… Georgian… not in a very good state, but you've seen about everything else in your price range…." He let his outstretched empty hands finish his sentence, and as I left his office, he didn't bother with his roguish wink.

The memory of his words stopped me in my tracks. "Price range." The price. I couldn't remember that he'd mentioned it and there was nothing on the papers I held in my hand; just a grainy black and white photograph of the house, apparently taken in the pouring rain, and managing to reduce its beautiful Georgian lines to those of an old workhouse.

Now I'd reached the house and stood on the wide granite step, looking toward the front gate, and could almost see the girls playing there, hearing their laughter as they ran in and out of the trees. There'd be a lawn, a few flower beds, perhaps roses.

The man had given me a large bunch of keys, saying without enthusiasm that he thought one or two of them "should fit something." I was pleasantly surprised when the first key I tried easily opened the front door, revealing a square hall with the remains of an old-fashioned woodblock floor.

As I looked toward the stairs I experienced that same earlier feeling of familiarity with the house, and decided to go up and count bedrooms. Luckily I looked at the stairs before starting to climb as several of them were splintered away to almost nothing.

So instead I made for the door at the far end of the hall, which must surely lead to the kitchen and possibly old storerooms. When I opened the door and went down three steps, I first came to a butler's pantry with the lingering smell of apples. Next to it was a large cloakroom, followed by two smaller rooms and a broom cupboard.

I made a mental note that if we ever moved in I must disconnect the bells for summoning the no-longer-existing staff. I paused to get the feel of the place, and... you were there, although that first time you were little more than a sensation, the feeling you get when you know someone else is in the room. How long had you been there, waiting for me?

Later, there came a time when I visited art galleries and hunted through old prints trying to find where you fitted in. From your clothes you might have been around for over 150 years, which tied in with the deeds of the house, and probably made you the first tenant. But it wasn't important. You were no ordinary ghost.

Happily, in spite of my fears, we managed to get a mortgage and moved in, after a few essential repairs had been carried out by an appallingly inefficient builder. Then came the business of what to call our new home. As the girls pointed out, "How can you call a house 'Mountview' when there isn't any mount?"

And they certainly gave it every chance, balancing precariously as they peered out of every window. But there wasn't so much as a glimpse of a mount. So "Mountview" went out, and "Lane End" came in.

The night of the renaming, I went into the corridor by the butler's pantry to tell you about it, hoping you'd approve. You didn't say anything, but then you never did. And after I'd spoken, you stayed quite still, your stillness giving you a reassuring air of self-possession, which was always there until the day you saved Katie's life.

All that morning I'd been aware of your presence close by, each time I went into the kitchen. But for the first time I detected an uneasiness about you, and asked if there was anything I could do to help. As usual you remained silent, and I continued to feel your disquiet.

Then I found myself with too much to do in too short a time. I put lamb chops under the grill for the twins' lunch, before strapping Katie into her highchair in the kitchen, while I hurried into the sitting room for something. I should have been aware that there was possible danger in a kitchen where the electric cooker was jammed up beside the only exit, but I'd got used to various shortcomings in the old house and no longer worried about them.

The moment I went into the sitting room, the phone rang and as it was a friend I hadn't spoken to for a while who seemed in need of a friendly ear, I forgot about the lamb chops cooking and Katie sitting in her highchair and settled down for a chat.

I heard the twins racing up the gravel drive on their bikes, and waited for the front door to be pushed open and for them to come running into the house, shouting each other down, competing for my attention, each wanting to be the first to tell me what had happened that morning at school. At this moment passions always ran high.

"It's *my* turn to tell her. You told her first yesterday." Blows would be exchanged. I promised my friend I'd phone her back, and went out into the hall to try and keep the peace, but before either of the girls had a chance to speak, I became aware of someone behind me, and turned to see you in the doorway at the end of the hall.

Your body was contorted, as though in pain; your mouth open in a silent scream; there was terror in your eyes.

I careered headlong past you, smelling smoke, which came swirling out of the kitchen as soon as I opened the door, all but hiding Katie from view. Although she was coughing, she clapped her chubby hands in delight at the spectacle of the cooker engulfed in flames. I saw out of the corner of my eye that you were still close by me as I rushed Katie through into the hall and handed her over to her sisters.

"Take her out into the fresh air," I told them before hurrying back into the kitchen where I doused the flames with a washing basket full of damp clothes — probably not the recommended method, but I didn't have time to think. And, thankfully, it worked.

For some days after that there was no sign of you. Then one Sunday lunchtime, I was in the kitchen, passing plates through the serving hatch into the dining room, when I saw you standing by the dining room window. For some reason, seeing you there unnerved me.

"Get out of there at once," I bellowed, and a German student who'd recently moved in with us looked dismayed. "No. Not you." My attempt at an explanation only made things worse and the student soon made her excuses for returning home.

But what was far, far worse was that you went too. No warning; just your absence. Perhaps my loud shouts had offended you. Perhaps you felt you'd earned the right to move into the rest of the house.

Some weeks later, I was having coffee in the house next door with my elderly neighbour when she asked me a question that took me by surprise: "Do you feel happy in the house?"

"Very. Why do you ask?"

"Well, apparently there was a terrible tragedy in there, years and years ago; a fire, a real inferno, and the father of the family couldn't get to his little daughter, through the flames and smoke. He had to watch helplessly as she burned to death."

"So that's what happened," I heard myself say, then seeing the startled expression on my neighbour's face, changed it to "Yes. I can imagine."

"They say," she went on, "that that family — probably the first to live in the house after it was built — was terribly unlucky. Their eldest son died while mountaineering, which was why — I believe — the house was called 'Mountview,' to show the family always kept him in their thoughts."

No wonder you left. How insensitive we must have seemed, changing the name. It makes me all the more grateful to you. Of course, I still have questions. Why did you only appear to me, never to the rest of the family? And why did I feel so strongly that something was wrong the day you left the back of the house and I saw you in the dining room?

You've never returned and I shall never know the answers. And now it's our turn to leave. After many happy years in "Lane End," and with the girls on the point of leaving home, we sold to a young couple with a family, much as we were when we first moved in.

And you? I only hope that your absence from the house is a good sign, my nameless, frock-coated friend, that it was your grief that chained you to the house, and that was why you called us to come there. Wherever you are, I wish you well, and earnestly hope that by saving someone else's child from the terrible death suffered by your own, you have been able to leave your prison forever, the scene of your almost unbearable loss, and find peace at last.

Ever since she was a child, Angela Vale has written stories and poetry. She was introduced to the possibility of meeting people from beyond the grave by a favourite aunt of hers, who was a spiritualist.

Angela is a professional actress who trained at RADA, then worked in a repertory theatre, where she met and married her writer husband, Adrian. His work took them to Ireland, where Angela ran her own theatre with friends. It was also where she met her "Silent Man." As well as acting in theatre, TV, and radio in Dublin, Angela co-wrote and performed in several revues there, and wrote a weekly column for a woman's magazine.

On returning to London, she gate-crashed a West End audition, and went on to play Mother Peter in *Once a Catholic…* and went on to do many other theatre and TV shows, recently working with the Royal Shakespeare Company.

In spite of having five daughters, Angela has always found time to write — poetry, short stories, and several novels (one of which, a romance called *Enter a Stranger*, has been published).

Diving into the Supernatural

by Kevin Wright
New York, United States

It was a hot August day in Kingston, Ontario. The sun beat down relentlessly, all but broiling me in my neoprene wet suit. I wiped away a bead of sweat as I made final adjustments to my gear. In just a few short minutes I would cool off in the chilly waters of Lake Ontario, as I descended eighty feet below the shimmering surface. We were moored above the wreck of the *George A. Marsh*, an old three-masted sailing schooner that made its final journey across the lake on August 8, 1917. I've dived on wrecks many times before, but this was my first visit to the *Marsh*. The pre-dive preparations went so smoothly, almost routine — little did I know this would wind up being unlike any dive I had ever experienced.

After a final equipment check I positioned myself on the gunwale of our small boat, took a breath from my regulator, and rolled backward into the placid waters of the big lake with a gentle splash. Surfacing quickly, I gave the signal that all was well and swam to the mooring line where I would wait for my dive buddy to join me. Bobbing ever so gently on the surface, I thought about how unusually calm the waters were today and how different it must have been on that fateful night almost eighty-four years earlier when the final voyage of the *George A. Marsh* ended on the muddy bottom.

Slipping beneath the surface, the hiss of air venting from my buoyancy vest was abruptly replaced with a watery silence, interrupted only by the sound of my own breathing during the slow descent to the grave of the once-proud ship. Looking up, I watched as the surface grew dimmer and ever more distant until it faded away into a brown nothingness. For several minutes we would be in that zone of emptiness, where the six- to ten-foot visibility permitted us to see neither the surface nor the bottom and making the thin nylon mooring rope our only proof of the existence of a world beyond the range of our own vision. After what seemed like an eternity, the form of a ship slowly materialized beneath me. Initially just a distant specter, the ship grew clearer and clearer until finally I stopped my descent, coming to a hover just above the deck of the good ship *George A. Marsh*, claimed by the lake so many years ago.

Pausing for a moment to take in the ethereal scene unfolded before us and to become acclimated to the icy cold water, we made our way slowly back across the hull. The ship was exceptionally well preserved, almost intact, with nothing to indicate that it had been there for more than eighty years — except for the thick colony of zebra mussels and other marine life that encrusted every inch of its wooden surface. Fish, surprised by our sudden intrusion into their watery world, darted past and then cautiously circled back to investigate our presence. Looking to my right, I saw my dive buddy deeply engrossed with a line that led from one of the deck cleats over the side. As he carefully studied the tangled rigging, I made my way to the back of the 135-foot-long ship.

We shouldn't have become separated like that, especially on an unfamiliar wreck. However, we were both highly experienced divers. In fact both of us were scuba instructors, and I was also a commercial diver, so the "buddy system" sometimes meant diving the same body of water on the same day. Thus, I found myself alone, exploring the lost secrets of the nineteenth century schooner that succumbed to the forces of the lake on a stormy August day within sight of its intended destination. Surveying the damage to the battered stern, I reflected on the tragic irony — this ill-fated ship had crossed the lake, riding out the brutal storm, only to perish within two miles of port.

Working my way forward, I came across one of the open hatch covers exposing one of the three cargo holds. I peered inside curiously, my dive light reflecting off fine silt particles suspended in the turbid water as a school of small fish hovered above the nearly full load of coal sitting undisturbed after so many long years. As I continued my journey back to the bow, I paused at each hatch and, opening it carefully, looked into the darkness while trying to steal a glimpse of the history that lay before my wondering eyes. Finally, I came across a large hatchway leading below deck. In a momentary lapse of judgment, and throwing safety to the wind, I decided to penetrate the wreck. Checking my air, I saw that I had just less than 2500 psi remaining. I took a compass bearing and then carefully descended, headfirst, into the inner sanctum of the ship.

The interior was a paradoxical scene of chaos and order; debris was strewn about on the silt-covered floor, yet pans sat undisturbed on the stove. It was totally dark inside, except for the trickle of dull light coming through the open hatchway and the powerful but narrow beam of my dive light. As I looked around, exploring what remained of Captain Smith's seagoing home, I suddenly developed a sense of general unease. Fearing an equipment problem, I immediately began to check my gear only to find everything in perfect order. My nervousness grew, my breathing quickened, and I realized that the water was quite cold, much colder than I had noticed before, causing me to shiver despite my thick wet suit. The light slipped from my shaking hand, fell to the deck, and went out, leaving me in total darkness. I suddenly sensed I was not alone, even though I had noticed no fish or any other sign of life inside the schooner.

On the verge of panic, I frantically groped for my light, yet my hand found nothing but silt. Forcing myself to calm down, I retrieved the backup light from a pocket in my buoyancy compensator vest. Inexplicably, this light — which had worked fine when I tested it earlier — no longer functioned. Going back to my vest pocket, I quickly pulled out a Cyalume lightstick, snapped it, shook it, and was rewarded with the expected comforting greenish-yellow glow. Using the light of that chemical glow stick I found the dive light I had dropped earlier — right next to what appeared to be a child's foot!

I gasped with shock at this unexpected discovery and, thinking I had found the remains of a modern drowning victim or the body of a murdered child hidden away deep inside the submerged wreck, I debated whether I should look up, doubting that I wanted to see the grisly spectacle before me. Tentatively, cautiously, my eyes traveled slowly up the leg until I saw the pale form of a boy about seven or eight years old. His clothes were not waterlogged, his hair didn't look wet, and he was standing firmly on the deck without any appearance of floating. As my disbelieving mind tried to process this bewildering scene, the figure of a woman appeared. She looked to be in her thirties with long flowing hair and a long skirt, and she cradled a baby in the crook of her arm. Like the boy, she appeared quite normal, but pale, and she didn't seem at all wet despite being more than eighty feet beneath the water. We stared curiously at one another, my eyes riveted to these mysterious figures. As if paralyzed, I was transfixed by the manifestation of this unusual sight and yet strangely relaxed. I had no sense of time and didn't even think to look down at my watch. Then suddenly the woman took the boy's hand, he smiled at me, and they were gone.

Still not sure of what I had just seen, the sense of panic returned. After checking my air gauge, to my horror I found I had just over 200 psi remaining. I hurriedly exited the wreck, swam to the mooring line, and ascended as quickly as I dared to without risking decompression sickness. Arriving at 15 feet, I hovered at the decompression safety stop until my remaining air supply was exhausted. Quickly swimming up the final 15 feet, I broke the surface under the bright midday sun and gasped in a big breath of fresh air.

Safely back on the boat, I was visibly shaken and recounted to the others this strange tale. Despite having logged thousands of dives, I have never encountered anything like it before or since. I initially chalked it up to purely physiological factors. Perhaps it was a case of nitrogen narcosis — the so-called "rapture of the deep" — though I had never experienced narcosis that intense or at such a relatively shallow depth. Maybe it was a result of cold, stress, pressure, claustrophobia, isolation, darkness, or a combination of these factors. However, later that night, while telling the story in a local waterfront bar, another, more ominous explanation was offered.

According to some of the older locals, grizzled old sailors, this was not the first time that ghostly apparitions had been seen on or around the wreck of the *George A. Marsh*. It seems when the ship went down on August 8, 1917, she took twelve of the fourteen souls aboard to their deaths. Those killed included two men, three women, and seven children, one of which was an infant. Rumor has it that to this very day Captain Smith, his wife, and five of their children still stand watch aboard the three-masted schooner *George A. Marsh*, eighty feet beneath the surface of Lake Ontario.

Kevin M. Wright is the owner of Inland Marine Construction Corporation, a commercial diving company based in upstate New York. In addition to making working dives, he is also an avid recreational diver who particularly enjoys teaching entry-level scuba classes and exploring the pristine wrecks beautifully preserved by the frigid waters of the Great Lakes. In addition to diving, Kevin also enjoys flying small planes, restoring 1970s Trans Ams, and outdoor activities including boating, fishing, and hunting. He writes as an avocation, a labor of love that provides him with a creative outlet. Kevin is especially fond of writing about diving and the underwater world, as he feels that the power of the written word enables him to unlock the secrets of the deep and to share with his readers a magical place that covers more than 75% of the surface of our planet, but that fewer than 1% of the population will ever have the opportunity to experience for themselves. He welcomes comment and can be reached at kwright@inlandmarineconstruction.com.

The Old Country

by Ann Howard
Sydney, Australia

My Nana was from Ireland, "The Old Country" as they called it, and was respected in our family for having "the sight." Some of the things she said made you smile, like "be careful of people with brown eyes," or "don't trust anyone from Cornwall," or "be careful of people who come to the house on Thursday mornings." Life was quieter then, and only a few people came knocking at your door, but she usually knew who it would be. When the spirit was upon her though, nobody smiled. Her eyes were dark pools and her old mouth a grim line. She would wave her hands over the tea leaves in someone's cup, sigh, gaze for a long, long time with her hooded eyes, and tell the most amazing things.

Funnily enough, she didn't know when her husband was going to be killed. He had been a head gamekeeper to the Duke of Bedford and did very well (two for the Duke's table and one for ours!), so he was able to leave his service and buy a small house in London. He tried living like a gent but was too wild. He was in trouble for driving a pony and cart while under the influence of alcohol in the High Street of Leyton and disrupting the traffic. After a brief appearance in court, where he made the magistrate laugh, he decided to join the Army.

He was killed two years later on a campaign in South Africa, leaving my Nana with a house full of children to care for on a small army pension. Neighbours and friends would come to the house to have their fortunes told and leave a loaf, some fruit, or eggs or potatoes, so we ate well, although we wore hand-me-downs and often had bare feet.

Of all the nine children, Lennie was her favourite. Perhaps it was because his health was not so good. He had occasional asthma attacks and was never as strong as the others. She always pushed the best bits of food his way and he sat on her lap near the fireside when she was telling stories to the other children around her feet. When World War II came along, Lennie decided to join up. Nana threw her apron over her head and begged and cried at the news. She had five sons going but she cried for Lennie.

Lennie was away for three years of that terrible war. Nana would talk about the boys often but she always finished with, "Oh, but my Lennie."

I was at her house one sleepy afternoon in autumn. It was the day before my birthday, October 8. The sky was a dark silver. Smoke curled lazily up from the bonfire of leaves in the orchard. Nana was dozing by the fire in her rocking chair, an old patchwork shawl around her shoulders. The kettle was hissing softly on the red coals, the cat purring. A mist hung around the house and the setting sun looked like powdered glass. I was lying on my stomach on the rug doing a jigsaw puzzle, enjoying the warmth of the fire along one side of my legs. The old clocked ticked slowly, but it was as though there was no time at all.

Suddenly, Nana started from her chair, her arms and fingers rigidly in front of her, dark eyes fixed on something terrible, sobbing, "Stop. Oh, no. Stop!!"

The cat's fur stood on end and I watched from the rug, amazed.

"What is it, Nana?" I asked.

She beckoned me to stand by her chair, holding out her shawled arms and held me close to her. "Lennie. Oh, my Lennie," she sobbed.

I was frightened and started to sniff and cry.

"Wisht," she wiped my tears away with the fringe of her shawl and soothed me.

I grew up and became engaged and married. My husband was an accountant and liked things properly done. When I tried to tell him about my Nana, he frowned and I kept quiet. We went away to our own home and I didn't see much of my Nana for over two years, but I was there when Lennie came home from the war. He was the first to return. The others were with Wingate in Burma and stayed away, serving until 1945.

The house was cleaned as though royalty were coming. Lennie put his head around the back door and took us all by surprise. He had grown and was tanned. He had lost his asthma. Nana's face was a picture, beaming and shining, with the odd tear escaping. She didn't know whether to feed him, wash him, or put his clothes away. Even the old cat was purring.

Nana made a great dinner for us all. Later, we sat quietly, Nana and Lennie and me. My husband had gone to get some more beer and my sister was running a bath for Lennie. The others were putting the wee ones to bed.

"How was it, son?" Nana asked softly.

"Not so bad," Lennie pursed his lips and nodded. He continued, "There was one strange thing, though. Out of all of it, I remember this day and I'll never forget it. We were in France. The bigwigs were well back and I was in the frontline. I'd seen many killed and wounded and every day that you got through was a miracle. The mud was like toffee, it tore at your feet. There were rats everywhere. We were cold, we were frightened, and we couldn't turn back. Some tried it and were shot by their own.

"I was advancing on foot with my mates across this terrible patch of ground. We'd been told to take a small ridge ahead of us with two stunted trees on it. We didn't know why, we just knew we had to. We were in an advancing line, shoulder to shoulder. Suddenly I saw two arms with rigid fingers sticking out straight, coming up out of the ground toward me. They were so real that I halted and stumbled. The other men continued and they ran into a line of hidden mines. The mines exploded and when the dust cleared, I was the only one still alive."

There was a silence. "Do you know what day it was?" asked Nana, her dark eyes fathomless, her mouth a slit.

"Why, it was October 7th, the day before this young chick's birthday." He patted me on the head.

I looked at Nana and the look on her face was something I am still searching for words to describe.

Ann Howard is a grandmother who was born in England but lives in Australia. As you can see from her picture, she enjoys life but assures the reader that this ghost story — and "The Lady on the Verandah" — is absolutely true. Ann is a frequently published fiction and historical nonfiction writer.

A Venice Ghost Story

by Nancy Spavento
Venice, Italy

As a dewy-eyed newlywed I had moved to the town my husband, Giovanni, came from, none other than the romantic city of Venice. Here I began a brand new life, gradually easing myself into the social scene thanks to my work as an English teacher which led me to mix with Venetians from all ranks of life and social class, right across the board from talented glassworkers to pastry cooks, stevedores, and professors of medicine. It was exhilarating working out different ways to communicate with such a range of people and it opened many new doors for me. My life quickly became a whirl of thrilling engagements as the legendary Italian hospitality became reality and my husband and I were "guests of honour" at many a dinner in a Venetian *palazzo*.

One balmy summer evening this year, a good few years since my arrival in town, we were returning from a late al fresco dinner on a friend's magnificent roof terrace in the leafy square, Campo San Giacomo dell'Orio. It had been a memorable event with plenty of laughter and high spirits. We took our leave well after midnight, though things were still raging.

In true Venetian style, the two of us were traveling by rowing boat, a slender wooden craft known as a *sandolo*, with just enough room for an oarsman aft and a passenger seated fore, whose responsibility was to hold a torch and act as a navigation light, warning other boats of our presence. In addition to the marvelous atmosphere and smooth dark water gliding by, it meant moderately relaxing post-prandial exercise. Without the worry of being pulled over for a breathalyzer test, most evenings we would scull along the quiet waterways and moor right outside our home.

That particular night Giovanni was doing the lion's share of the oar work, as the standing-up rowing technique means you need a good sense of balance — not my forte, especially after a series of superb wines!

We decided to take a different route back to enjoy the cool night air and headed along a side canal, Rio di San Zan Degolà. It was especially peaceful, quite a contrast to the chaotic party we'd just left. I was settling down on a cushion at the front of the boat when all of a sudden it felt as though we had entered a bank of fog. An eerie, damp chill spread over us both, and I wrapped a shawl around my shoulders but couldn't help shivering all the same.

It must be a trick of the wind channeling through the narrow canals, we imagined. Apart from the tinkling splash of the oars as they dipped into the dark water, the only other sounds were the odd gentle meowing of a lone cat and the soft calls of the seagulls that paddle around on the water in search of scraps in the evening once the heavy boat traffic has gone.

Or so we thought. The cries became rather louder and more persistent the further we penetrated the ever-darkening waterway, and began to sound like the smothered cries of… children. Plaintive, thin voices could be heard uttering the words, barely distinguishable, "*Aiuto! Aiuto!*" "Help! Help!" How could this be? All around were forbidding walls of decrepit buildings, which seemed to be growing higher and higher. Not a sign was there of an opening or alleyway, let alone a window. We looked at each other in rising alarm without speaking a word while Giovanni increased his rowing efforts. My hands were trembling and the torch I was clutching jumped around, causing a weird effect of faint unworldly lights reflected off the water, and doing nothing to reassure us as the spine-chilling calls gave no sign of ceasing.

Thankfully, it wasn't that long before we emerged into the brighter lights of the broad expanse of the Grand Canal itself, and we breathed sighs of relief to be away from those scary sounds and unsettling atmosphere. As the current was quite strong here we pulled over to the side, close to the ferry landing stage of Riva di Biasio, before the final leg home.

Though it scared me at the time, I didn't think much more of the incident (and hesitated telling friends as I was afraid of being ridiculed as a "hysterical foreigner") until some months later when we were indulging in our habitual Sunday lunch at my mother-in-law's.

Signora Elsa was commenting on how things had changed in Italy in general and what it meant to grow up in Venice in the animated Rialto market area where the family had a vegetable stall. Life had been good, she said, despite the shortage of food, as there were few restrictions on the children. Just the odd "out of bounds" rules like keeping away from boats and not hassling the shopkeepers.

Reminiscing further, Elsa happened to mention that she and her companions would never play in the vicinity of the Grand Canal embankment Riva di Biasio. When I pressed her for an explanation, the old lady confided that the parish priest had issued a dire warning concerning evil forces. My immediate "rational" explanation for this was as a preventative measure to stop them from drowning in the infamously strong currents at the turn of the tide. Then the strange sounds from that summer evening came to mind....

My curiosity aroused, a few days later I found time between English lessons to pay a visit to the library to read up on local history and, lo and behold, uncovered the terrible tale of Biasio. A butcher in medieval Venice, he did a roaring trade in the flavoursome sausages for which he was renowned... until a customer complained to the authorities that he'd found a segment of human finger in one. It turned out to belong to a child. An investigation revealed that he had in fact been concocting his wares using the flesh of the young children he enticed into his premises with promises of sweets. Unsavoury remains were soon unearthed in his cellar. The authorities promptly escorted Biasio in chains to the scene of his crime where they unceremoniously chopped off his arms. This was followed by beheading and quartering in St. Mark's Square.

Needless to say, his butcher's shop was completely razed to the ground by enraged citizens. Nothing at all remains today. But guess what else I discovered in the accounts? It all happened in the year 1503. Exactly 500 years ago! So were those pathetic voices and cries for help we heard that summer evening those of Biasio's tender-aged child victims... or just a distorted echo effect, common across the water after dark, as the locals would have it?

Australian Nancy Spavento has been lucky enough to live in the romantic Italian city of Venice since 1981. As well as teaching and translating (at the prestigious Venice Film Festival), she works as a travel writer and photographer, and has researched and written ten walking guides to mountainous (and flat) parts of Italy as well as a city guide to Venice itself.

The Shoe Thief

by Jade Walker
Washington, United States

I have ugly feet. It's true. I had great feet until I was about four years old. That's when I decided to become a dancer.

Ballet. Tap. Acrobatics. Jazz. Modern. I took classes for years, all with the hope of becoming the next Debbie Allen or Mikhail Baryshnikov. All those years at the barre studying my movements in front of an entire wall of mirrors damaged my feet into the mess they are today. In my teens, I had two foot surgeries, both of which left scar tissue.

Not a pretty sight.

Needless to say, I don't wear open-toed shoes or those cute, strappy sandals women are so fond of in the spring and summer. I don't get pedicures and I wear socks all the time. Shoes are my friends.

My ugly feet have rarely been spied. I'll occasionally show them to a boyfriend, but only after I'm sure he's fallen in love with me (and thus can get past my whole disinterest in toe-sucking).

My best friend Amy saw my feet too, but even she only saw them after years of companionship. So imagine my surprise when in 1999 she stole my shoes from me. I was particularly shocked by this act because she'd been dead for several days when it occurred.

Ames and I used to visit this tiny beach in Florida called Gulfstream. Whenever we wanted to unstress or unburden our souls, we'd visit this private oasis on the Atlantic Ocean.

Normally, she'd take off her shoes (she had perfect little feet), and we'd walk down the sand to a rock dune. This rock sticks out over the ocean and is fairly uncomfortable to walk on when barefoot. Of course, it was never a problem for me since I always wore shoes.

We'd scramble up onto the rock and look out at the horizon. We'd cry and hug or laugh over the idiotic things we'd done when triple dog dared. Once in a while, we'd rid ourselves of the trappings of love or dream of a shared future — a future that was never meant to be.

I'm not a religious person, so when Amy unexpectedly died, I simply couldn't deal with all the farewell trappings of eulogies and viewings. Instead, I paid my respects to her parents and then drove out to the beach.

I walked down to the water and across the sand over to our rock dune. It was warm and sunny — typical Florida weather for a February — and I found myself angry at Mother Nature for not providing more appropriate weather. Perhaps I was just mad at the whole situation.

I stared at the horizon and silently called to her. I demanded an explanation for her death. She was only 28 and we had huge plans she needed to fulfill.

Who was going to fly to New York City with me for the millennium on New Year's Eve? She and I had been planning that trip for eight years. Who was going to be my maid of honor when I eventually got married to the perfect man? Who would be there for me to shock and surprise, and share the secrets no one else would understand?

The sounds of children playing, dogs barking, and water rushing toward the shore faded as I stood on that rock and silently screamed into the ocean's ear. Grief overwhelmed me, but I simply wasn't able to exorcise the sheer agony I was feeling.

I needed something to ground me, some way to keep from having a breakdown. I opted for physical pain. So I took off my shoes and tenderly placed my ugly, sensitive feet onto the rock.

The stones were uncomfortable, but not unbearably so. Once I realized that I couldn't even share this moment with her — this silly little moment of independence from shoes — I started to cry.

Amy was never one to let me dwell in depression. As someone who had endured a kidney transplant, years of painful medical procedures, and more than one broken heart, her mere presence always reminded me of how small most of my problems were. No matter how much my life would suck, hers was always worse. Somehow, she never let it stop her from smiling and living life.

The tears fell in continuous streams and I was blinded by them — so blinded in fact, that I didn't see this huge wave heading straight toward me. It crashed over the rock and into my body, almost knocking me off-balance.

With one hand, I reached down to pull my wet skirt away from my calves. The other I used to wipe the tears from my eyes… and was just in time to see the wave steal my tennis shoes and pull them away!

I couldn't jump in after them; it was simply too rocky and dangerous. Instead, I was left helpless, friendless, and shoeless.

I was also quite stunned to hear the sound of Amy laughing. She had this infectious giggle and I heard it clearly in the ocean breeze. My skin prickled, and I knew her ghost was there.

As always, because she laughed, I did too, and with that shared chuckle, I said farewell.

I constantly mourn for Amy. Not a day goes by where I don't think of her, or wish her to be on the other end of the phone. So much has changed in my life since she died, and yet, I would trade it all for just one more day with her.

Some people are never able to get past the death of a loved one. They wear their grief like a shroud and find it difficult to cope with the regular tasks of living.

If I were to behave in such a manner when she was alive, Amy would have pummeled me. Or, more likely, she would have forced me into the car with the stern prescription of a few hours at the beach. Knowing Ames, she also would have stolen my shoes so I couldn't leave until I felt better.

Jade Walker is a freelance journalist, the editor of *Siren Song Magazine*, and the writer behind *Jaded Writings and The Blog of Death*. She is also the former overnight editor/producer of The New York Times on the Web, and the former editor-in-chief of *Inscriptions Magazine*, which won four awards from *Writer's Digest*. To date, she has published several books, including the dark poetry collection, *Sex, Death and Other…* (2002, Metropolis Ink).

The Chalice

by Margaret Walker
North Wales, Great Britain

The Communion vessels clanked as my husband, Michael, prepared the bread and wine for the Wednesday morning Communion service. It was held in the small Lady Chapel of his West Yorkshire church in the North of England. I looked up to see if he had spilt the wine. Normally one of the parishioners laundered the altar linen, but if he was responsible for the spillage, the job would come to me.

Other members of the small congregation had looked up too, but all was well. I closed my eyes for the prayer of consecration — a luxury afforded to me only on Wednesdays. On Sunday mornings the children would be with me in the pew and I couldn't risk closing my eyes for more than twenty seconds at a time. Vicarage children had to be seen to behave in church!

Mrs. Shaw was at this service. She was a homely looking woman in her late sixties or early seventies and had recently moved to the parish to live in an upstairs flat of a large house very close to the church. It was built of the same millstone grit, which had once been a pleasing grey, but had been darkened by the ravages of smoke from the mill chimneys. By the 1970s there were scarcely any mills in the town, which was now a smokeless zone. The area to the west, on the edge of the Pennine Hills, was the most salubrious and pleasant part of the town.

The church, the vicarage, and Mrs. Shaw's flat looked out onto seventy acres of open parkland — a favourite place for dog walkers, cross-country runners, and model aeroplane enthusiasts. At the weekend it was a mecca for football and rugby teams. From the church the road climbed gently uphill to the grammar school, which had once been an orphanage, built, of course, in the same millstone grit, but in an ornate French style. The houses by the side of the park were opulent Victorian dwellings; behind them ran smaller terraces, criss-crossed by even smaller ones of much more modest means.

The congregation, like the houses, was an affable mix. On this particular Wednesday in April 1979, Mrs. Shaw invited a few of the parishoners to her conveniently placed flat for a cup of coffee after the service. My husband had shaken hands with her as she left the church and I overheard her asking him, "Who was the gentleman helping you at the altar today?" adding, "I didn't notice him until I looked up when you clanked the chalice." When Michael told her nobody had helped him — he had a server only on Sundays — she looked at him in a curious way. She obviously believed that there had been someone there. "He was by your side," she said. "He was trying to tell you something." Michael tried to assure her again that he had been alone in the sanctuary, and he left her to enjoy a cup of coffee with her friends and hopefully clear her mind.

So convinced was Mrs. Shaw that she had seen somebody that she described him in detail to a long-standing member of the congregation who immediately recognized him as being a former church warden who had been held in great esteem in the parish, but who was now dead. Frank had been a server at the altar, and had lived in one of the smaller houses behind the large ones on the edge of the park. Mrs. Shaw hadn't been perturbed by the news that the visitor to the sanctuary was someone who had been dead for several years. What did perturb her was that he had been trying to communicate with the vicar, almost as if he was wanting to warn him of something. But of what? And when and where? She laid the matter, and the ghost, to rest as she cleared away the coffee cups. She hadn't known this man. Nobody else had been aware of him. The vicar had denied having anyone to help him at the altar that morning. And in any case, what could be done if no one knew what the communication had intended to convey?

The next morning, Michael was called out to help at a service in the neighbouring parish where the vicar was ill. Our children were at school, so I went with him. On our return, as we drove down the side of the park, or "the moor" as it was known locally, we saw a solitary shoe on the grass, surrounded by a blue cordon and an alarming number of policemen.

By noon it was common knowledge in the area that there had been a murder. A young girl of nineteen had been killed most brutally in the early hours of that morning as she had walked home from her grandmother's house. The one o'clock news revealed her name. She was a girl from our parish, and had lived in one of the small, terraced houses near the moor. She was the eleventh victim of the so-called Yorkshire Ripper.

The following morning I met one of the ladies who had been at Mrs. Shaw's coffee party. Until then I had no idea of the identity of the mysterious visitor at the altar. He had died long before we had arrived in the parish, but this lady sincerely believed it had been Frank. And now she knew why he had come and what his warning was. I was intrigued, but more than a little cynical. But this lady was like a dog with a bone and would not rest until she had regaled me with Frank's life story — whom he had married and where he had lived.

Back at the vicarage, Michael was preparing to visit the murdered girl's bereaved parents and brother, who had once been in our church choir. "Where do they live?" I asked.

The answer, like a thunderbolt, laid flat my cynicism.
It was the house where Frank had lived.

Margaret Walker (nee Jefferson) was born in 1940 and brought up in Yorkshire, England. After four years at University in Nottingham and Durham she qualified as a Medical Social worker, and in 1963 married Michael, who had just started work as an Anglican Curate in York.

During the ensuing forty years Margaret combined her role as wife and mother of three with an active role in her husband's churches, first in urban parishes in England and then in rural areas in North Wales. She acted as his secretary and parish clerk, led meetings, did pastoral visiting, and enjoyed speaking to women's groups.

For nine years she worked on religious programmes for local radio stations and hospital radio, both as an interviewer and a contributor to "Thought for the day." This work inspired her to do more writing, and she has now had several articles published in British magazines.

The daughter of a piano teacher, Margaret plays the piano, organ, and folk harp, and participates in dancing in many forms.

Now in retirement with her husband and their sheepdog, Rhian, she lives in an old sea captain's cottage above the harbour in Porthmadog, North Wales, and has time to write more prose and poetry, as well as to indulge in watercolour, singing, and computing.

Margaret is currently engaged in writing her autobiography, much of which will focus on the fourteen years she spent in West Yorkshire, the scene of this story, "The Chalice."

My Grandmother's Visit

by Scotty Hughes
Auckland, New Zealand

I had always been very close to my grandmother. She had lived with my parents and me for all of my fifteen years. As a teenager, the closeness remained; I'd accompany her on shopping trips and she'd usually treat me by allowing me to buy some of the latest records.

In August 1973 she went into hospital for what the family thought would be a short visit. We later found out through messages she had left us that she knew she would never come home. She may have been prepared for her death but we weren't, and it wasn't until she went into a coma a few days before her death that we accepted the inevitable. When she passed away at the age of seventy-seven in September, we were all devastated, especially me.

Two weeks later I still hadn't settled down or accepted her dying, and I was finding it hard to concentrate on schoolwork. One morning I was lying in bed, tossing and turning in the early summer humidity. My grandmother was very much on my mind. It would have been about 3 A.M. I finally began to drift off to sleep when my grandmother materialized in front of me.

I recoiled in shock, not believing what I was seeing. She touched me gently on the shoulder. I was stunned by her appearance in more ways than one — she no longer looked sick but radiant. She looked as she had looked about fifteen years before. She smiled at me, with her head slightly tilted to one side in that old familiar way. She spoke to me and told me that there was no need to fret — she was fine and no longer in pain.

She was reunited with my grandfather who had been the love of her life. She had married him as a young girl of seventeen and he was forty-two. When she was widowed in her thirties, no man was ever going to take his place and she never remarried. After consoling me, she told me she had to leave me and would never be coming back but she knew now I'd be okay. She slowly backed away from me, gently waving the way she used to do to departing visitors, until she vanished.

I lay in the darkness for what seemed an eternity, my heart beating so rapidly it was almost to a Motown music rhythm. Eventually, I climbed out of bed and switched the light on. Emotionally, I was shaken, I was scared out of my wits by what had happened, but part of me was strangely calm. I'd just had confirmation that life does continue on after death.

Finally I dropped off to sleep, only to awake with a start. My first reaction was to check the clock but the room was now in darkness. It was just after five when I went and woke my parents and asked them which one had turned my light back off. They both denied even leaving the bed all night and went back to sleep. In the morning I staggered out, bleary eyed, and told my mother what had taken place. One of the first questions she asked was what my grandmother had been wearing. I felt a chill run down my spine, like someone had stuck a pile of leaves down my back, smothered in early morning dew.

I hadn't noticed before, but my mother had on the very same pale blue cardigan my grandmother had been wearing. My mother told me that it was a cardigan my grandmother had bought on her last shopping trip.

Grandmother had tucked it away at the bottom of a drawer. She had never got the chance to wear it before going into hospital, so I had never seen it in my life. It had stayed in the drawer until that morning, when for some reason she wasn't quite sure of herself, my mother had decided to remove it from a pile of clothes in the drawer and wear it.

It was one of the strangest experiences I've ever had. It convinced me that there is a world where the dead live on, a place where they are contented and all previous pain ceases. I'm sure that the only worry in the afterlife comes from the departed being concerned about those left behind, hence the visitations people receive.

In my grandmother's case we had been so close and she worried so much about everything going on in my life, I don't think she would have been at peace until she had reassured me everything would be fine. I feel that she was demonstrating to me that one day we would be reunited.

I will always be grateful for her action in coming to check on me, the gentle manner she reassured me with, and the stroking of my hair. It gave me the comfort I needed to move on.

The best part of the whole experience was the way in which it altered the last impression I had of her. When she died, she had been in a coma for a week. Although it was a peaceful death, there were still signs of previous suffering on her face that all the skills of the funeral director couldn't entirely remove. The coldness also played on my mind. She was the first dead person I had ever seen or touched and I retracted hastily from that texture, so much like marble. When she visited me, I'll never forget the warmth that was back in her hands and how the lines of pain in her face had evaporated. I was given a gift in that I now have in my mind the smiling, gentle familiar face, rather than the stranger's face I saw at the funeral home.

True to her word, she never returned. As far as she was concerned she had completed her last duty.

When my wife was dying in hospital seven years ago, one of the first things she said to me when she came around was that I wouldn't believe who was standing in the corner watching over her. It was her grandfather who had died two years before. After my experience all those years ago I wasn't surprised at all. There is something very comforting in believing that the people we've been closest to in life watch over us in death.

My grandmother's visit convinced me of it. I've often wondered what it would be like to receive a return visitation and have a conversation together as two adults. Maybe I'll have to wait a while longer for that privilege. I did have expectations of making contact again when I paid my only visit to a Spiritualist Church. Instead, my wife's first boyfriend made contact, but that's another story.

I am a recently qualified freelance journalist, just dipping my toes into this brave new world. I reside in Auckland, New Zealand and am forty-five years of age. Before getting into journalism, I ran my own small manufacturing business for nineteen years. It kept me on my toes but I had the desire to do some writing and thought it was now or never. So after enrolling in a journalism course I came out the other end with a diploma in Freelance Journalism.

On a personal level, my hobbies include CD collecting; I now have over 1,000 and around 4,000 45s. I'm into the nostalgia thing, collecting music from the '60s through to the '80s. I enjoy watching most sports, especially horse racing. If I hadn't left it so late in life I would have loved to have been a pro horse trainer. I also follow rugby, which is huge in this part of the world, and cricket. I also collect videos and DVDs and like nothing better than sitting down with my partner, Lynda, and watching a movie. Taking part in pub quizzes is another pastime I enjoy. We have a team that gets together on Wednesday nights. We don't do that well, but have a heck of a good time in the process.

Living with Ghosts

by Don J. Rearden
Alaska, United States

It's a simple fact that nearly all the old school buildings in any Yup'ik village in Southwest Alaska are haunted. The old Bureau of Indian Affairs teachers probably started the rumors, the stories, the fear mongering. Then parents and the elders played to the tales, telling the kids in hushed voices that to play outside after dark meant, "Monster will get you."

This was especially true of the rickety old school buildings in the village I lived in for a year, the structure standing above the tundra on hundreds of black steel legs driven deep into the permafrost. For a good scare the kids would run under the buildings at night, knowing that any one of a hundred different monsters or ghosts might grab hold of them and steal away into the darkness. Sneaking into the buildings after dark was a whole different beast. The ghosts of dead teachers roamed the long hallways, and books fluttered like white ravens through the classrooms. Everyone, from the elders to the toddlers, conceded the old BIA buildings were haunted. The old red school my family moved into in the fall of 1988, in Kasigluk, Alaska, was no different.

Our apartment, a converted classroom with a kitchen, living area, bathroom, and two bedrooms, sat off the side of a long dark hallway that connected the school building with storage facilities, abandoned teachers' quarters, and the generator house. The long buildings were connected with what I can only describe as a terrifying series of above-ground tunnels. Perpetually frigid, the long enclosed hallways made your breath puff out like smoke on even the warmest of days.

Our living situation, for a family of five, was less than perfect. But all things considered, we had the second-best house in the village next to the principal, who probably lived there from the time the first white men came with their vodka and Bibles.

My two younger sisters took one bedroom and I the other. My folks, having already sacrificed their friends and family back in Montana for the move north, sacrificed their privacy and made the living room their bedroom. Our first day in the place, I scouted out the building as best I could. At the age of twelve, and a devoted Stephen King fan, the place reeked of mystery and intrigue. I ventured down the long hallways and poked my head into the different dusty buildings that were unlocked, never leaving the safety of the long hallways, and never closing any doors behind me.

After my first night in our spooky new home, I headed outside into the glaring tundra sun and made my first friend, a little guy with spiked black hair and a pleasing giggle. "What's your name?" he asked, only it came out as all one word, something like "whach-yer-name?"

I introduced myself. "I'm Donny."

He continued the quiz, "Where you from?"

I responded as if he could grasp the notion of how strange my old home was from this place. "Montana."

He giggled for no reason and I joined him.

"You see any ghosts in that place?" He nodded his head toward the school.

I shook my head. "No. You?"

The boy lifted his eyebrows and smiled, a Yup'ik gesture I would come to know as "Yes."

He took me to his house, a small one-room plywood structure with a large color television, a small wood stove, one bed, and a table. Several small kids were playing on the plywood floor and his mother sat at the table doing beadwork. She looked up from her beading when we entered. I still didn't know my new friend's name, but I picked it up when she said, "Yago, take out the bucket."

He responded to her in Yup'ik. I caught a bit of my name amongst the frenzy of dancing "Q" and "K" words that filled the small house. His mother sat her beadwork down and looked me over, "I used to help cook lunch at Akiuk. So scary that place is."

I understood that Yago had told her we lived in "Akiuk," the old school building.

That night I mulled over the implications of living in a house that everyone thought was haunted. In the safety of our cozy apartment, with my mother and father sleeping in the room next to me, creating a nice buffer between my room and the hallway, I drifted off to sleep wondering just what made the place haunted.

In the months that followed I began to get a grasp on the extent of the haunting happening in my home. Sometimes we'd hear footsteps sauntering down the dark hallway, past our apartment, knowing that it was just the janitor, but then we'd hear the roar of the janitor pulling up on his snow-go a few minutes later. Or hearing the familiar sound of a ball bouncing in the gym at the far end of the building, only to peer out from the safety of the apartment and down the long hallway at the inky blackness of the empty gym. Then the lights to classrooms would be on in the middle of the night. Or a window would be open during the middle of a howling tundra blizzard.

It didn't help that my father took a job in Bethel, some thirty miles away, leaving me as the man of the house during weeknights. This job I held with pride, but at night when the generator would suddenly shut off and the alarms would shriek throughout the building, I was often too terrified to accompany Mom down the long hallways to reset the generator. I'm ashamed of having her take that awful trip alone, while I sat with my quaking sisters, all of us certain she'd never return. The generator almost always shut off during the darkest, coldest nights. The screaming alarms tearing us from restful slumber, reminding us we lived alone in someone else's home.

Fittingly enough, my first physical encounter with a spirit happened on Halloween. We didn't have a telephone in our apartment; the only phone was down the long hallway and in the office. Once in a while we'd hear the phone ring and one of us would go tearing down the long, green tile floor in our socks to grab it on the last ring. On this particular night, I managed to grab the phone just in time. It was a girl who had a crush on me, and I sank into one of the office seats and began to work my magic on her. In the rush, I'd left the office lights off, but the hallway lights were on, and seeing I was playing the part of the village Romeo, I didn't have time for spooks.

While we talked, of what I cannot begin to recall, my eyes moved around the familiar office. From out of nowhere, a drawer in the large gray filing cabinet at my side suddenly rolled open. My heart froze. My gut lurched. I blurted out a frenzied, "I gotta go — bye," slammed down the receiver, and sprinted down the hallway to the safety of our apartment. Once inside our house, which was impervious to the ghosts and ghouls that roamed the school, I slammed the door and threw myself against it. Out of breath, my heart still not quite functioning correctly, I relayed to Mom the horror that had just graced my presence. Without missing a beat, she told me the drawer always opened like that and they usually kept it shut with tape. Of course this came as a great relief to me, and I felt quite childish, though I didn't go down to continue the phone conversation for several days.

Mom could dispel all stories of ghosts and haunting with simple science. She had a knack for it. The windows opened because of pressure created by the wind. The lights came on and off from the irregular power from the troublesome generator. The abandoned teachers' quarters weren't used because they had asbestos. The stories of the black principal who died on Halloween were just told to scare kids and keep them out of the building, just like the stories about the teacher who hung himself in the storage room. All of the so-called hauntings, according to Mom, had been cleverly crafted to keep kids out of the building when school wasn't in session. And when I thought about the dozens of kids who lurked around after the final bell rang, or the kids who asked to visit us day after day, only leaving when Mom said, "It's time for you kids to go home," it all made sense to me. The explanation had to have some ring of truth to it. Why else would kids not want to explore and vandalize a half dozen vacant buildings?

My months of living in a building that even most of the village men wouldn't visit after school hours became a sort of revelation to me. As much as I wanted to believe in the supernatural, I found it possible to explain away everything. The mystery and the intrigue with my house became blasé. I turned away from the fear of the sounds, and lights, and alarms, and began to focus my attention more heavily on the cuter girls in the village and on exploring the tundra with my new hunting partners.

At age thirteen, I had reached a critical juncture in my life. While I respected the spiritual beliefs of the Yup'ik people and became enthralled with their stories, I dismissed my own beliefs in ghosts and spirits. I wanted to believe, and I loved to tell my own scary stories, but in my heart I knew they didn't exist.

Now, nearly fifteen years later, I know they do. I know that the tales, each story related to me about the building, had its own bits of truth. A principal did die there of a heart attack — during a Halloween haunted house, no less. Another teacher did hang himself there. Maybe some of the light problems and the windows opening and closing can be explained away by science. Maybe the bouncing basketballs were just balls placed haphazardly on the ball rack, left to fall off and bounce wildly across the floors from simple gravitational pull. Maybe the generator's sudden power failures in the middle of the night were merely fuel flow problems, always remedied by a simple flick of a switch. At any rate, my change of heart came a few years ago over a late-night discussion with my mother.

We were talking about being scared, and I asked her if she remembered that night when I saw the filing cabinet open and how terrified I had been. She nodded and smiled, like only a mother could. Then she proceeded to recall that event, and the numerous other events that year; all those hauntings and stories that she had systematically and methodically dispelled.

She smiled again across the table, her eyes narrowed like they were peering down those long, dark hallways. "That year was the scariest year of my life. Some nights, when you kids were already asleep, I'd lie there in my bed with my covers pulled over my head like a little girl, hoping I'd fall asleep before I heard footsteps in the hall. Some nights I'd wake up and all the lights in the entire building would be on, and the windows — all wide open."

Dumbstruck, I heard myself asking, "What about that filing cabinet?"

She nodded her head, remembering my fear, remembering her own fear, remembering her simple motherly lie. "After you told me about the drawer, I went down the hall and closed it, and taped it shut. I didn't want you to be scared in your own home."

I have spent the majority of my life in the wilds of Alaska. All hours not spent outdoors are, of course, devoted to creative pursuits. My first feature film is due to be released sometime in the summer of 2004, tentatively titled *The Unknown*. I'll graduate from the University of Alaska, Anchorage with my MFA in Creative Writing next December. I've published in a variety of rarely read and obscure places, and won several awards that make my mother proud. I am fortunate in having my writing habit supported by my beautiful wife, Annette, and also incredibly lucky to have assistance from my mentor, Daniel Quinn, author of *Ishmael* and *The Story of B*.

There's No Place Like Home

by Gail Kavanagh
Queensland, Australia

When I was a little girl, Belfast was the sort of city where strange things were expected to happen.

There was a kind of sinister mystery about the place, quite chilling to a happy-go-lucky Corkster like me. Born in the free South of Ireland, I found the North a trying place at the best of times — the political air of Belfast always seemed oppressive.

My parents' work often required us to stay a week or so at a time in Belfast. Usually, we stayed at a friendly guest house, with a jolly couple who loved children and cooked mountains of sausages for breakfast.

I was about eight when we had to go there for a week on short notice. With our favorite guest house booked out, we had to settle for a couple of rooms in a newly opened guest house nearby. Our former landlady gave us the address but seemed reluctant to do so.

The woman who owned the guest house was called Moya. She said we were her first customers. Her father had recently died and left her the house in his will.

"I have two rooms," she said, looking at me. "Do you want a separate one for the little girl?"

Dad consented and we walked up the narrow stairs. As soon as I walked into the room she designated for me I started shivering. The weather was warm for that time of year but the room was deathly cold. There was a thin, hard-looking bed in one corner, and the grate still had the remains of a dead fire in it. But there was something more than that, a feeling of dread that hit me like a cold, damp blast of air as soon as I stepped inside.

"What's up?" Dad asked, seeing my stricken face. I shook my head and backed out of the room.

"She can sleep in our room," Dad said. He glanced around the cold bedroom, at its bare neatness, the comfortless bed, and the ashes in the grate.

"The old man slept here?" he asked. Speechless, the woman nodded.

"How did you guess?" she inquired.

"It's a man's room," he said, adding under his breath as he ushered me out, "a bitter old man."

We settled in, with me sleeping on a pallet in the room my parents had been given. This room was at the front of the house and seemed more cheerful. Moya said it had been the master bedroom when her mother was alive, but that her father had moved into the back room after the funeral.

"I often said we should let it out," she said, "but he wouldn't have that."

No doubt, the house was a strange one. I felt someone following me all the time. Once I spilt milk in the kitchen while making my parents a cup of tea. I mopped it up and left the floor clean again. But all the while I had the feeling of being watched by disapproving eyes. On the stairs, I walked up with my back flat to the wall. Even going past the old man's room filled me with dread.

My mother appeared not to notice any of this, but my father seemed very aware of everything, and I told him how the house made me feel.

"Don't worry," he said. "I'm watching out for you."

That made me feel better. In our family it was said that my grandmother Bridget had the Sight, the ability to see beyond the thin veil that separated this life from all that lies beyond. She often said, with a secret smile, that two of her children had inherited the Gift. I knew now that one of these was my father.

One night, a few days after we arrived, I woke up in fright. There seemed to be a disturbance in the room, and I heard my father's voice, speaking softly, but very stern and angry.

I sat up and gathered the blankets around me. The room seemed very still now, but I also felt strangely calmer, as if something had gone from the house.

I heard my father's voice say calmly, "Go back to sleep, Gail, everything will be all right now."

He was right. After that the presence never bothered us again. The old man's bedroom still seemed a cold and bleak place, but it no longer terrified me as I went past the door. But even with the calmer atmosphere in the house, I was still very glad to leave at the end of the week and return to the South of Ireland.

Once we were over the border, my father pulled up at a cafe and while we enjoyed a cup of tea and some sticky buns, he told us the real story of what had happened at the house. This was all news to my mother, who hadn't noticed anything paranormal, although she did say she found the atmosphere in the house oppressive. But for me a mystery was solved.

On the night I had awakened in fright, my father said, he himself had been wakened a little earlier by the sensation of someone trying to strangle him.

"I opened my eyes and there was an old man hanging over me... he had his hands around my throat and he was screaming at me to get out, leave his house, or we would all suffer."

My mother's jaw dropped... so did the penny.

"It was Moya's father," she said.

"That's right. He was angry that she had turned the house into a guest house. He had made her promise not to do that before he died."

"I can't believe this. I slept the whole time," my mother said. "I never heard a thing. What did you do?"

"He was an old man and already dead, so I figured I couldn't hurt him," Dad grinned. "But he was strong... I pushed him back and got out of bed and told him that we were staying and if he did anything to hurt my family I would come after him. Right into the next life, and I would hunt him down and send him to Hell."

I was goggle-eyed. "Weren't you afraid?" I asked.

"No," Dad said. "The dead are nothing to be afraid of. I told him he should be finding his wife again instead of hanging around trying to ruin his own daughter's life." He rubbed his throat. "But I didn't know the dead could be so strong — maybe I was just a little surprised by that. But I was angry too... and he didn't want me coming after him into the next life. So he left."

My mother, who was English and spent all of her time in Ireland trying to convince herself there was no such thing as ghosts, banshees, and all the other spirit beings the Irish took for granted, shivered.

"Why didn't you tell me?" she demanded. "We would have left the next day."

"I know," my father said. "And he would have done the same thing to the next people who moved in. I had to show him he couldn't get away with it. That's why I didn't tell you what had happened."

A memory suddenly flashed into my mind. "But you did tell Moya," I said.

"And how do you know that?" he said, his eyes twinkling.

"Before we left the house she shook your hand and said thank you."

Gail Kavanagh was born in Ireland, and now lives in the land down under, where the women glow and men thunder — but only in the cricket season.

She has been a working journalist for ten years for an Australian Newsltd company, and still works part time as an entertainments reporter. Her freelance activities include writing for the web and print publications and making the transition to creative writing.

Online credits include Fables, Spark Online, Oralin (an astrology column), and short stories in print publications such as *Family Circle*, *For Me*, and *Australian Playboy*.

Clips of Gail's work and links to related sites can be found at http://www.geocities.com/gailkav/.

Visitor at Shiloh

by Mona D. Sizer
Texas, United States

My great-great-grandmother Comfort Annis was a witch.

To be a witch or a Granny woman at the time of the Civil War could be a dangerous thing. Perhaps not so much in the Tennessee hills where people lived with signs and "portents," where "ha'nts" stalked the ridgelines and "will o' th' wisps" flitted in the low places, and when the fog settled in the valleys and rose again without warning, it left bare things no living, breathing, God-fearing soul should see.

In the Tennessee hills people were more accepting of "powers." They were more superstitious than we are today. And less ignorant of the other truths.

Even as a child, Comfort Annis knew things no child her age should know. Her pale blue eyes were the color of the streams and could see just as clear. Her own mother wavered between being proud of her daughter's knowledge and punishing her for saying saucy, knowing things. After only three years of schooling, her own father decided she'd had enough and should stay home doing housework and tending the livestock. Idle hands were the devil's workshop, he always said.

Gradually, she came to realize that she was different from her brothers and sisters. When she heard tell of three powers of an old Granny woman over on the far side of the next mountain, it was as if her mind had opened a door. She didn't know what she was supposed to do with what she found inside, but she knew she was supposed to step in.

The first time she was sure, a neighbor came wailing with her baby for Comfort's mother to help her. The woman laid the tiny, limp burden wrapped in a little appliquéd quilt on the hearth close to the fire. She turned to wring her hands and beg for help while her husband stood in the doorway, all sulks and disapproval because they'd disturbed Comfort's father. An argument started. The woman cried; the man snarled. The family tried to soothe the troubled waters.

For a minute the baby was forgotten. Comfort edged close and then closer. She knelt and unwrapped the little face — so blue with tiny feet and hands all cold. While no one watched her, she took the little face between her hands and blew into the baby's nose and mouth. She murmured words from the Good Book that fell from her lips without her thought. Unbidden, she recited them three times.

And the baby caught her breath and whimpered.

At the sound all four heads turned at once.

"Here! Get away from there!" the man cried.

Comfort turned her pale eyes on him.

He shut his mouth sharp and hard as a bear trap. His wife rushed to gather her baby daughter up in her arms, laughing and crying all at once as the baby hiccupped and cried too.

Comfort's father stood back and stared, but her mother darted forward and caught her daughter by the shoulder. With a sharp spank to the bottom, she sent her up the ladder into the loft where her brothers and sisters lay listening in their beds.

There in the dark, she listened to her father explain with an uneasy laugh that the heat from the fire had warmed the baby up, and Comfort had just waked her up when she'd patted her cheek. It was easier to accept that explanation than look for the truth.

Another time she found she could stop blood from flowing.

Her brother cut his big toe nigh off chopping wood. His face white and tear-stained, he came hobbling to the house and collapsed on the porch.

"Sister," he whispered, all but passing out with his foot hanging off the step and spattering blood over his mother's white and yellow daisies. Their mother was in the spring house. Their father was plowing.

All alone they looked into each other's eyes. She untied his ruined shoe and pulled it off. Peeling back the bloody sock, she clasped her hands over the wound. Her gaze never left his as she began to whisper verses from the Good Book. The first time, he raised his head. The second time, he sat up. The third time, he repeated the verses with her. He reached down with his hands and covered hers. Together they said the verses three times more. And the bleeding stopped entirely.

They sat real still for a long time. She took her hands away and stood.

"You mustn't tell," she said.

"I promise not to," he said. He looked at the end of his leg. "I guess I'll have to lose those shoes."

She nodded and hastily stood up and stripped off her bloody apron. They could hear their mother coming from the spring house. "Bury this with 'em."

Fire was the most frightening gift of all, for it came to her and went from her. She could lay her hands on a person with a fever and repeat verses three times. Her palms and fingers would burn as if they were laid on a stovetop. The skin would turn red. Sometimes a blister would pop up on her fingertip or the heel of her hand.

The person with the fever would cool, but she would be blazing hot, red in the face, nigh on to convulsions.

"Never speak of it," her mother said. "Never tell a living soul what you can do. This is not your place. It's for God and His Son. You're an unworthy vessel."

"Even if somebody asks me for help?"

"'Specially if somebody asks you for help."

But people came to know. One person told another. Another told another. People in terrible pain, bleeding, nigh unto death came to her in the middle of the night. Sometimes, despite her mother's warnings, she did what she could.

When she married, she hid her powers from her husband, Thomas. He was a good man who steered his course by the world as revealed by his five senses. He gave her children — three daughters and two sons.

And then on the first of April, he went away as a Tennessee Volunteer in the Union Army. He marched twenty-nine miles down the road with the men from Wayne County to the ferry at Pittsburgh Landing. It took him across the Tennessee River. From there the volunteers deployed into the woods and meadows east of Shiloh Church and into some of the bloodiest fighting of the Civil War.

Not even the generals really knew what men were where. Sometimes, the Union soldiers didn't know whether they were shooting at the Rebels or their own men. The woods were thick. The roads crisscrossed each other. Soldiers might think they were on Purdy Road only to discover they were on Eastern Corinth Road marching or galloping to collide with the enemy.

The mightiest collision took place at a slaughter called Hornet's Nest.

There the battle raged all day as the generals poured more men into the field until the ground ran red with blood. The Union lined cannon up in a peach orchard to the west and fired grapeshot to cut wide swathes through the attackers. They didn't really know whom they were firing at. They just followed orders.

From the porch where she sat shelling peas in the heat of the afternoon, my great-great-grandmother saw the first soldier coming from the battle. He was gaunt. His face and clothing were black with powder smoke from the cannons. He'd tucked his hand into his belt to support the weight of his arm. A dried, rust-brown stain covered his whole sleeve from the ragged hole even with his armpit. She reached for the squirrel rifle beside her chair, but he wore parts of a blue uniform and he was clearly no longer a danger to anyone.

As he stood swaying in the dooryard, she offered him a drink of water.

He was the first of many that trailed by. She couldn't do much more than give them water from the well. She stationed her six-year-old son, my great-grandfather, to lower the bucket as it emptied. She herself passed the dipper, then rinsed it after each man had a drink. She had no extra food to offer. Her winter's larder of carefully preserved and canned victuals was almost gone.

All day she waited, but her husband did not come. She had asked about him, but no one whom she had helped knew anything. Even the few men she recognized from Wayne County could not remember seeing him in the long fight that had gone on with such noise and confusion from nine in the morning.

Comfort began to be more and more afraid, sure that Thomas needed her, sure she needed to go. As the hot afternoon wore on and no more wounded soldiers trailed by, she put the children in the house and locked the door. She stationed my great-grandfather at the window with the rifle poking out between the sill and the sash. At the other window was his five-year-old brother with a broom-handle poking out. She drew the shades and told them all to be quiet as mice.

Then she saddled Thomas's horse, a gray so old he was nearly white. She filled a canteen, put food, bandages, and her Bible in a towsack, tied her bonnet down tight, and galloped westward toward Pittsburgh Landing.

The noise of the cannons made the horse difficult to hold as she neared the landing. From the Tennessee River the Union gunboats *Lexington* and *Tyler* blazed away, shattering the trees along the banks to reach the soldiers in gray.

The ferrymen wouldn't take her across. "No, ma'am. Not a civilian." Though she begged and pleaded, they opined it wasn't a place for a decent woman. She thought about swimming the river, but her horse was tired. If she drowned, who would care for the children, locked alone in the house, two little boys bravely assuming responsibility for the day.

She thought about turning for home, but surely, surely Thomas would come. As the ferry crossed with the reinforcements and recrossed with the wounded, she scanned their faces as they were carried off. Her hands itched to touch their bleeding wounds, the terrible powder burns that blistered the sides of their faces.

Those who lay still on stretchers, she longed to touch and blow the breath back into their bodies.

But she could do nothing. Her helplessness galled her.

Gradually, the guns fell silent. The hoofbeats died. The ferrymen no longer brought many living men across. As they started back with the empty boat, she led her horse aboard, keeping it between her and their prying gaze.

On the other side of the water, she had to clutch her horse's bridle to keep from sinking to her knees. The spirits of the dead were everywhere. They brushed cold fingers against her cheeks and whispered in her ears. As if they had fled the battlefield and come up short against the barrier of the swift-flowing Tennessee, they weighed on her soul. She should have been afraid, but all she felt was a terrible sense of pity. They had died in such pain. They were so young, so afraid, so angry at being blown out of life.

But where was Thomas? He must still be alive. Surely, his soul would have sought and found her when she stepped from the ferry. She mounted the pale gray horse and started down the riverbank. At last they came to a road. As one she turned his bridle as he turned his head. This time she heeled his sides and clicked her tongue, sending him into a gallop.

Her bonnet blew back, but she rode straight in the saddle, her whole soul concentrating on Thomas. At the end of the road was a sight she recognized. It was the Hell described right down to the last detail by the Bible in her sack.

In the evening after the daylong battle, wounded soldiers, both Yank and Rebel, crept in from Hornet's Nest to find the nearest pond. At the sight, Comfort began to weep helplessly and hopelessly. In the rising moonlight, the place was rusty red. The bodies of men lay half in, half out of the water. The ones who had come to drink had been too weak to pull themselves back from the edge. They had drunk of the life-giving water and drowned as it closed over their heads.

As she stood on the bank, a mist began to rise from the pond. Like a veil it covered the horror, as if it were bestowing a blessing upon all their souls. Comfort began to pray. As she wept and prayed, wraiths rose from the undulating mist on top of the water. The air grew colder and colder. She began to shiver.

She must leave. The ferry would not make many more trips once darkness fell. She couldn't leave the children alone all night. She held out her arms. With all the fervor of her spirit she called silently to Thomas, loving him, and bidding him farewell. The mist stirred again, drifted toward her. She closed her eyes. She could not help him despite her powers. She would not look at him. Cold fingers touched her cheek; a spectral palm caressed her hair. The gray horse stirred restively, snuffled softly as if in greeting to his master.

"Thomas."

Then he was gone. She turned the pale horse and made her way back to the ferry and her orphaned children.

photo by Dorothea Pennington

The family legend of my great-great-grandmother's visit to Shiloh is absolutely true. Why would she lie? More important, why would Comfort lie to her granddaughter, who was my grandmother?

As a child I listened to these stories wide-eyed. To this day, I believe them implicitly. When my ten-year-old daughter and I visited Shiloh in 1975, both of us were struck by the aura surrounding Bloody Pond that lies between Hornet's Nest and Peach Orchard. So many men died there. If there is a single place in America more haunted, I would be afraid to visit it. Whether my great-great-grandfather drowned there is unknown. But Comfort Annis certainly believed that he did.

Later in the little museum, my daughter Rachel asked to see the final roster in the silver-gray book on the countertop. She turned unerringly to the lists of the Wayne County Volunteers and found her great-great-great-grandfather, Thomas Peyton Stanfield. The docent was flabbergasted. How could this child turn so quickly to the exact place and find the correct name with barely a glance? I truly believe the connections were made between them, and he became part of her.

For the readers who would like to know, Comfort Annis Stanfield rode safely home that night from Shiloh Battlefield. Her eldest son, James Wayne, my great-grandfather, had kept them all safe. After the Civil War, she reared her five children on a widow's pension of twenty-eight dollars a month.

The Belgian House

by Margaret Langley
Worcestershire, England

We had been lucky to find the house when we moved to Belgium in January 1974. At the same time General Motors was moving in and taking up all the best rented houses for their stay, so there was nothing much to be had. It was in a good area too, one of several houses built in the woods on the outskirts of Antwerp where my husband was going to be working.

It was a big three-story house, about seventy years old. A colonel in the Belgian army who had served in the Belgian Congo for many years had built it. He had built it in the old colonial style, nice big rooms with high ceilings and marble floors. Best of all, there was a balustraded veranda we could sit out on running the whole length of one wall. It had shallow steps leading up to the white painted front door and with its red pantiled roof and whitewashed walls, the house was a most attractive proposition. The large garden was overgrown with dense dark rhododendron bushes which had invaded the knee-high grass of what had once been a lawn, but we could soon cut that back. It had the advantage of being well away from any neighbours, so the kids would be able to play without disturbing anyone; there would be no complaints about noise.

There were three bedrooms. My husband and I had one and as they were still small and the rooms were so large, we put all three children together in one room for company. The other room was to be a guest room. We stacked away the suitcases and cartons in the small middle attic and gave the children the sunny south-facing one as a toy room. The staircase was a bit dark but I painted it white and I papered the toy room in a sunshiny yellow and painted the wooden beams bright blue. I covered the floor with a multicoloured rag-rug carpet, so it was cheerful and cozy. I planned to use the other attic room as a sewing room, but later, when I'd had time to fix it. It faced north and was damp and very cold and the wallpaper hung down like cows udders from the sloping ceiling.

I was really busy unpacking all the boxes and settling us into our new home. There was a great deal to do, finding a school for the children, locating the best shops, arranging for a teacher to come to the house to teach the children to speak Flemish so they could cope at school, and struggling with the linguaphone to learn the language ourselves. Any spare time my husband and I had left was spent working on the garden. It was some weeks before I realized that the children, then aged seven, five, and three, would never go alone to the toy room — always waiting for a brother or sister to go with them. Mike, our middle child, talked sometimes about Bart, who he played with in the attic, but then he had always had imaginary friends. So it was not until Grandma and Granddad came to stay that I began to take notice.

It was getting dark one evening when my mother-in-law came into the kitchen.

"Isn't it time that you took that little boy home?" she said. "It is nearly bedtime."

"What little boy?" I asked.

"The one who is playing with our kids on the top landing." I was puzzled. Karl, the boy next door, sometimes came to play but I had not seen him tonight. I went up to look but there were only our three there.

"Was Karl here?" I asked.

"No."

"Anybody else?" They looked guilty but shook their heads. A quick look round reassured me and I went back downstairs.

"You must have been mistaken," I told my mother-in-law. She was unconvinced. "It was a little boy," she said. "They were playing at dressing up."

It was a few nights later that I woke up and heard Granddad prowling about in the attics. I got up.

"Anything wrong, Dad?" I asked.

"No," he said, puzzled. "I went to the bathroom and thought I saw Sam on the top landing, but when I got up the stairs he wasn't there."

I checked the bedroom but both my sons were fast asleep in their beds. My little daughter was sleeping too.

"You must have been dreaming, Dad," I said.

Neither my husband nor I ever saw the little boy.

It was some time before I got around to stripping the walls of the sewing room. It was always so cold in there. I sized the walls and coated them with foil to damp-proof it, then I papered it over with a bright floral paper. But it was still too cold to work in comfortably. I had my sewing machine up there and a long box the kids called the coffin that I kept my sewing materials in. The children did not like that room; they dashed past it if the door was open and refused to come in to try on the things I was making for them, though they couldn't tell me why.

Then our son Sam broke his arm. It had been a bad break, and the anesthetic had worn off when we got back from the hospital and he was in pain. So I left him rolled up in a rug on the settee while I drove to the pharmacy to get the tablets to relieve the pain and stop his arm swelling inside the plaster. He was on his own, as I had left the other two with a friend while I took Sam to the hospital. When I got back some ten minutes later he was nowhere to be seen. I called his name and he crept out from his hiding place behind the settee.

"What are you doing there, Sam?" I asked.

"I didn't like the PE teacher," he said.

"The PE teacher?" I asked, mystified.

"She came in here," he said.

"Oh, Sam, you shouldn't have opened the door when Mom wasn't with you," I said, disturbed.

"I didn't," he said, "she came in the back." I went and looked but the back door was locked and bolted just as I had left it.

"What did she do?" I asked Sam.

"She came over to the fireplace and fluffed up her hair in the mirror."

"But there isn't a mirror over the fireplace," I said.

"She thought there was," said Sam.

"Where is she now?" I asked him.

"She just went into the air," said Sam. "So I hid."

Some time later when I was alone in the house one day, I was working in the sewing room, when I became convinced there was something in the corner behind me. The room, which was always cold, had become icy and the atmosphere felt so malevolent I didn't dare turn round. I left my sewing and fled downstairs. I must admit I was afraid to go back. After that I moved my sewing downstairs and kept that door shut.

As I said, I never actually saw anyone, but sometimes we watched door handles turn and doors open, but I saw no one come in. We became accustomed to the ghosts who shared our house, and apart from the sewing room, learned to live with them.

Nobody seemed to know anything about our house. Then

some years later, not long before we left Belgium, an old neighbour told me a bit about it.

"A nice family lived there," he said. "There was an old man, his daughter who was a teacher in the local school, her husband who worked at Mercantile, and one child. They were something to do with the resistance in the war. They used to hide people trying to escape from the Germans. One of the ones they hid was spying for the Germans and gave them away. They came and took them away one night. We heard they had been shot. Don't know what happened to the child. Bart, he was called."

I have always wanted to write. In fact the English lecturer at college suggested that I should, but I never seemed to find the time. Bringing up our three children while accompanying my husband, an engineer, on his postings abroad and learning to communicate in the languages of the countries we lived in took up so much time. We have spent more than thirty years living in Sweden, Belgium, Monte Carlo, Italy, and the Middle East. I have taught art and crafts and English as a foreign language to both children and adults in some of these countries. My most exciting job was teaching in a school established by the ruler of one of the Arab Emirates for his daughters and the daughters of his government ministers and religious leaders. Our family is now grown up, one son moved to Scotland, one to Canada, and our daughter to England. Three years ago we moved back to England ourselves and I started writing articles and short stories and have now been published in seven English magazines.

Looking for a New House

by Sabrina Cheetham
Bremen, Germany

When I was five, my mother was pregnant with her third child. Subsequently, a larger house was needed to accommodate our growing family. We lived in Dorset, a beautiful county on the south coast of England, and as Bournemouth, our town, had hardly been touched in the Second World War, most of the houses were very old and steeped in history.

My parents made arrangements with an estate agent, dropped my two-year-old brother off at our grandmother's house, and took me house hunting with them.

It was a sunny spring day, and we went from one possible new home to the next. My parents were probably growing weary by the fifth or so house, but I was too young to notice, and I remember how I rushed from room to room, exploring every nook and cranny, as curious five-year-olds tend to do. Alas, so far every single property had had some disadvantage, or my mother fell in love with one which my father hated, and vice versa. And so the search continued.

It was late afternoon when we drove past yet another house which had a For Sale sign stuck on a pole in its front garden. I remember the house clearly; it was pretty large and stood directly on the corner between two roads. One half of the top floor was round, which made it unusual, and the agent told my parents that the house had been built just under a century ago. It wasn't on my parents' list, but they were getting desperate to find something on my father's only day off, so we parked the car again and got out.

Our first impression was that the house was bright and quite nice. The kitchen had a lot of wood furnishings and my parents stopped in there to discuss the ins and outs of fitted cabinets with the estate agent. I went on ahead and explored the rest of the place on my own, as I had done in all the previous properties.

There wasn't much to see on the ground floor. The sitting room had a huge stone fireplace, but that had obviously not been used for quite a long time. Aside from that and the kitchen, the ground floor boasted a dining room and a study. Both were big and empty; there wasn't a lot of exploring to do in an unfurnished house. I remember that the ceilings were pretty low, though, and thought that maybe people had been smaller in the old days.

Soon I got bored of the ground floor and crept slowly up the stairs to have a look at the other rooms in the house. The adults were just making their way into the sitting room, but I didn't mind; I had wandered off alone in every house so far.

The master bedroom also had a fireplace, but it was much smaller than the one in the sitting room. There were three more bedrooms, and the ones on the side facing the roads were round, which I thought was brilliant. I ran along the curving walls, trailing my little hand along the silky wallpaper.

I could hear my parents slowly ascending the stairs as I went into the last unexplored room, the bathroom. It was bright white, had two sinks, a toilet with an old-fashioned tank and chain suspended so high above my head that I was unable to reach it, and a big, white, raised porcelain bathtub which stood on four silver feet on the tiled floor.

The feet were carved in the shape of what looked like lion's paws and I had never seen anything like it. Giggling, I walked over to the tub and looked inside.

Two young children stared up at me, what looked like a boy and a girl. They had dark hair and huge, pleading eyes. I stood still, too shocked to move, and stared back at them. It looked as if they were underwater, as they were wearing long white nighties that floated gently above their pale bodies. They were squeezed close together, and didn't move a muscle.

For what felt like an eternity I stood there and gazed at them. They seemed to be a couple of years older than me and I wondered what they were doing there in the bath. Were their parents looking for a new house, too?

"Hello," I said eventually.

Suddenly, they both started wailing, screaming for help.

Startled, I started to scream too, and ran out of the bathroom, slap into my mother. I grabbed her leg and refused to let go. I was absolutely terrified.

"Whatever's the matter?" My mother had never seen me so upset.

"I want to go home!" I wailed.

"We haven't finished looking around yet. We still need to look at the bath…"

"Don't go in there!" I shouted, interrupting her. "It's a bad place here, it's bad. I can feel it. I want to go home, *now*!"

"Don't be silly," said my father resolutely, "there's nothing bad about this place."

"What did you see?" My mother was stroking my hair, trying to quiet me. I was still sobbing uncontrollably.

"Don't want to go back in there!" I gasped as soon as I had enough breath to speak again.

The estate agent looked very puzzled, and in the end, she and my father went in to have a look while my mother stayed on the landing. I was still wrapped around her leg.

After a minute or so, they came back out and were still at a loss as to what had frightened me so badly. They hadn't seen the poor children in the bathtub.

"Did you... help them?" I managed.

"Help whom?"

"The children! There are two children in the bath, they wanted me to help them, but I... I couldn't!"

"Children?" My mother pried me off herself, and transferred me to my father's leg so that she could go and take a look. She couldn't see them either.

"Come back in with me and I'll show you that there's nothing there to be afraid of," she suggested.

I wouldn't go. I refused to go within three feet of the bathroom door, so my parents decided against buying the house.

We were all tired and sick of traipsing round houses by that time, so we got into the car and went home. I was still in shock, had goose bumps all over me, and was shaking like a leaf. I was glad to get back to the safety of my comforting bedroom.

The next day my mother had a phone call from the estate agent. Intrigued by my violent reaction to the bathroom, she had done a little research on the history of that particular house. My mother went pale as she listened to the woman recount her findings.

It wasn't until I was quite a few years older that my mother told me what the agent had said that day. In the early 1900s, a wealthy, respectable family had lived in what they had all called "The Roundhouse." The father, a successful businessman, had an excellent reputation. No one could have guessed how violent he was toward his wife and children behind closed doors.

One day he lost his temper yet again and drowned his seven-year-old twins, a boy and a girl, in the bathtub.

Sabrina Cheetham, 24, was born in Germany, but spent most of her life in Bournemouth, England. She has been writing ever since she was able to hold a pen, and has had both fiction and nonfiction stories and articles published in various magazines and web sites.

When asked about her work, she likes to quote Gore Vidal: "When I read my first book, I started writing my first book. I have never not been writing." She is currently working on her second novel.

The Silent Bird

by Paul F. Newman
Dorset, England

June 1944. Dorset, on the south coast of England, is preparing for D-Day. Thousands of Allied troops are ready to leave for the final assault on Hitler's Europe. The comparative peace of the green hills and fields will lead to blood and destruction on the other side of the English Channel.

None of this history was in the forefront of my mind as I traveled the twisting coastal road by bus on a summer morning fifty years later. Yet very soon an odd incident would make me wonder at the power of anniversaries and the apparent ability of commemorative celebrations to unlock the past.

The road between the seaside towns of Lyme Regis and Bridport in Dorset dipped and rolled before us as the local bus chugged on. It took a long time to cover the short stretch of miles, but the scenery was spectacular. The bus was a "double-decker" and I was seated on the top deck near the front.

We had descended a narrow valley where the hills rose on either side, pressing in close as the bus sped between them. We shaved past white-walled cottages and recoiled from the smack of overhanging branches as the driver negotiated hairpin bends with frightening expertise. A shudder of gears and we were climbing again, grinding upward with determination. I was relieved that the bus was more than half empty as I would not have bet too much on its chances of reaching the top with a full load. But this was just the passing anxiety of a stranger and motorist unused to traveling above ground level. Without doubt our able driver and the scattered bunch of local passengers had complete confidence in their fate and everyone seemed entirely serene, bouncing and swaying in the rhythm of what to them was the regular way of things. The bus pressed on. Slowly but surely the blue of the sky widened above as we wound our way toward it. We had almost reached the summit when the extraordinary happened.

Without warning, a shadow fell across the left-hand side of the bus, suddenly blackening out the sky and causing a gasp from those on one side of the upper deck. Above us, the silent underbelly of a huge World War II aircraft was passing at a frightening proximity. It was so close I instinctively ducked. In that split-second I felt that a great black bird had swallowed the sun and was winging onward to its last inevitable resting place. Surely this heavy plane was going to crash into the hills.

I looked to the other side of the bus to gain a better view, to try and identify any markings, to hopefully see it pass over the hilltop into safety. But we turned a bend at the same moment and the aircraft was momentarily lost to sight. The bus driver appeared oblivious of the plane and the near disaster, as were those on the lower deck and the passengers on the right-hand side of the upper one.

There was no sudden outburst of chatter, no animated pointing and moving in seats, except for the one or two people who were sitting by the windows on my side and who were now craning their necks in all directions. I was impatient for us to reach the summit so that we might see the plane again, and in a few moments we had turned the last uphill corner. But when we mounted the crest of the hill the sky was bare. The land stretched away on all sides in peaceful summer splendour. Tiny cows grazed in far-off meadows, the sun glinted on the sea… there was no plane, no crash, absolutely nothing on the horizon for miles around.

It was only then that the oddity of the event began to fully register with me. Essentially, it was the total absence of noise from the aircraft that had seemed so strange. The expected roar and thunder of a large warplane passing closely overhead was missing. It had been completely silent. Not even the rush of a back-vent of wind had disturbed the landscape below. And no aircraft would have been flying deliberately at such a low altitude unless it was in serious trouble. There had been something unsettling about it from the first, much more than the natural shock of a close, low-flying encounter. There was a fatalistic inevitability. A feeling of the cold silence of doom.

I am not a knowledgeable airplane spotter but I had little doubt that this was an old wartime aircraft of times gone by. I had squared the anomaly of its appearance in my mind with the fact that this was the D-Day anniversary year and many old aerodromes were open to the public around this area with surviving planes on show and occasionally flying.

Needless to say there were no subsequent news reports that a plane had crashed that day. There were no reports that such a plane should have been flying at all, especially so far to the west of the old military airfield at Warmwell in Dorset whose wartime connections were well-known. Was this an Allied plane that had crashed on manoeuvres fifty years ago? Had it been returning shot-up from France? Had it limped back across the Channel losing height, only to falter at the last hurdle and plow into the dark folds of the coastline?

My later researches revealed that several Lightning aircraft had crashed in Dorset in 1944 or had been lost in action over the Channel. The shape of the great silent bird in my memory fit the illustration of this particular American aircraft given in the reference books that I subsequently pored over. The little flat silhouette on the page was far from the awesome shadow that had covered the sky, but it was the same template. Although I would never know the identity of the individual plane, that this was its family I was certain. Anniversaries are hallowed events. The word "hallow" means to make holy. I wondered if this particular phantom plane had ever appeared before or whether it was the official sanctioning of its memory in a fifty-year commemoration of time that had caused its brief but startling manifestation. I don't know the answer. Neither do I know anything of its crew or its mission or its identifying insignia. But I know that I saw it as real as day, then disappear as swiftly and silently as it had come.

Paul F. Newman is an astrologer by profession who writes, illustrates, and teaches on the subject in England. A book of his astrological cartoons called *You're Not a Person — Just a Birth Chart* was published in 1999. He also gives written and telephone astrological consultations and can be contacted by email at pneuma@ukonline.co.uk.

Serenading a Ghost

by Kinbria Swan
Oregon, United States

Back and forth, day after day,
I rode a bike to the musical village of Doolin.
Back and forth, day after day,
I rode a bike down a haunted road.

It is my opinion that in some cases ghosts are uninvited and other times we encourage them to overstep their other-worldly boundaries. In my case, I think this ghost saw people pass by and by and never bothered to haunt them. He was used to mortals passing near his domain and knew of the veil that blinded us from seeing the spirit world. He probably lived his afterlife undisturbed until he was boldly invited to reveal himself to a naive tourist.

I was 24 years old and was finally discovering the big world around me. Ireland was cool and moist, but I didn't seem to notice. The wind violently blew my hair around my head, yet to me it was only a kiss from the elements. I was in a beautiful country about which millions of supernatural stories have been written, and my eyes and mind were always searching for evidence of what I had read.

It was the music that drew me to Ireland. I wanted to learn to play and sing the traditional music, and so I decided to rent a holiday apartment in Doolin, County Clare.

My apartment sat at the top of a steep hill. I glided my bike down this hill every day, pausing a few minutes at the bottom. I looked curiously at this lush and boggy area which had a very strange feeling about it. I have always been sensitive to energy changes, and in this place, I could feel a dramatic change in the air. Although I didn't see anything white or monstrous, I was certain that I was being watched by a spirit.

Being the nice girl that I am, I decided to serenade whatever spirit lingered in this field. After all, music is an international language. You can travel to any country and by singing a song, you can connect immediately with the people. I assumed it could be the same in the spirit realm. Everybody likes a good song, right?

Yes, that is absolutely right! Or so I found out...

No, I don't blame this spirit for being intrigued by a little girl who stopped her bike, and without seeing anybody, sang for an invisible and hopefully interested audience.

No, I don't blame this spirit for following a happy whistling mortal up the hill to her apartment. After all, friendly neighbors are supposed to visit, aren't they?

Yes, it is in the rulebook of Friendly Neighbor Etiquette, "to welcome a newcomer to the block within the first week of arrival." I had always been delighted when a reader of the Friendly Neighbor Etiquette book stopped by to give me homemade cookies and say, "welcome to the neighborhood."

Now I was in a foreign country, in a lonely apartment, and I hoped that a redheaded local or two would bring me some shortbread or a bottle of Baileys Irish Cream. I longed to hear an Irish accent say, "Ye are welcome. 'Tis nice to have a Yankee in the neighborhood. De ye tink yee'll settle in Doolin?" Unfortunately, I didn't meet any redheads in Doolin, I bought my shortbread at the post office/food store, and the only bottle of Baileys I drank was at the pub.

It is no surprise then that sometimes the visitors you expect aren't always the kind that come. Okay, maybe they wouldn't be redheads, but I thought they would at least be mortal!

It was a windy night. The pub had been filled with mesmerized tourists, dancing and clapping along with the fiddle, whistle, cello, and accordion. It was a long and exciting session of music that seemed to put everyone into a happy, diddle-ee-i-dee trance. I too, felt the lingering magic from the music as I strapped the cello to my back and hopped on my bike.

The rain fell on my woolen hat as I raced up the blackened country road. I paused, as usual, to sing a little song for my invisible audience in the bog and then quickly rode up the hill to my cold apartment. I didn't even bother to light a fire this night. I went straight to my bed, snuggled into the duvet, and fell sweetly asleep.

We have come to the part of the story where I must ask you readers a question. Do you remember ever feeling like someone was watching you? Maybe you looked and looked around you and couldn't figure out who it was, but you knew that someone's eyes were on you. Do you know the feeling of your space being invaded? Someone comes to stand quietly behind you, you haven't seen them approach, yet you feel their energy invading yours.

Our bodies are remarkable the way they react to the possibilities of danger. For instance, when we touch something hot or sharp, without thinking, our body pulls our hand away. Not only does our body react when it is experiencing danger, it also gives us instinct or premonition, so that we have a warning about potential danger. These were the instincts that abruptly woke me out of a wonderfully deep sleep. Not only did my body boldly awake me, it continued to hold me under its intuitive control by not letting me react in any fearful way.

I could hear the breathing and could feel that its face was only three inches from my own. I was on the very edge of the bed and knew that it stood just beside me. Large round eyes were curiously staring at my sleeping face. It studied my mouth, nose, eyes, hair, and breath. I knew that I shouldn't change my breathing pattern. I knew that if it realized I was awake, it would go away.

I thought to myself, *this is me breathing, now this is something else breathing.* I heard my breath, then the spirit's breath, then my breath again. I timed the breathing for about two minutes, convincing myself of this encounter, and thinking, *I won't doubt this when I wake up. I'm not going to dismiss it as a dream, because I'm here timing the breaths and feeling the spirit's face only three inches from my own! And yes, I am so scared!*

Once I was absolutely certain of this ghostly encounter, I let my fear get the best of me. I didn't move, but I let my breathing change into a rapid, fearful pattern. The spirit obviously realized that I was awake and I could feel it slowly back away. It seemed to take a few slow steps back, pause a second to take one last look at me, and than hurry backward to where the floor meets the wall. It seemed to soak into the floorboards, and all I could hear was my own heavy breathing.

I lay awake for the rest of the night. I was in shock and fearful that it would come back.

I understood what had happened to me. I had naively given a big and friendly invitation to the ghost in the bog. Of course, I didn't think it would ever show itself, but why shouldn't it? I only lived up the road, I was friendly, and I sang to it several times a day! He'd obviously followed me to my apartment and politely waited until I was asleep to get a good look at me. Maybe if I hadn't freaked we could have had a good chat over a cup of tea, or whatever a ghost likes to drink. Maybe I ruined my chance for a phenomenal and strange relationship, but I was too unprepared to step into that realm. My advice is that unless you are very prepared and educated about the otherworld, you never mess around with it.

I lay awake in bed, thinking these thoughts, and watching the sky grow pink. I don't know why, but we never think ghosts will appear in the day... and so I let myself drift back to sleep. I awoke in the early afternoon and prepared to go to Doolin as usual. I hopped on my bike and rode swiftly down the hill, but this time I went as fast as I could past that haunted boggy field!

Kinbria Swan (Kimberly Stimmmel) was born in America in 1974. Kimberly changed her name to Kinbria Swan in 2000 for lyrical reasons. She explains, "I think it sings like a poet's name should. Like a sweet sound that flies off the tongue, floats into the air gracefully, drifting along in peace and pleasure." Kinbria has been singing and writing since a child, and has entertained thousands of people... both alive and ghostly.

Kinbria is fascinated with traditional music and writing styles. She studied American literature, poetry, and songs, and eventually found herself curious and excited about the foreign arts. She first traveled to Ireland in 1993, where she studied the music, writings, and culture of the Celts. Kinbria wrote "Serenading a Ghost" after having a curious encounter with a bog ghost in Ireland. She has a love for travel and cultural study and continues to visit and research other European countries. She incorporates these foreign influences into her musical and writing projects. Kinbria's traveling and creative adventures inspired her to write a poetry book titled *Poetic Secrets.* In it she reveals her innermost self — loving and inspired — as well as painful secrets in more than one hundred original poems. Kinbria has also recorded two Celtic albums, *Song Secret* and *Dreaming.* She has performed her music and sold her albums to thousands of tourists visiting Ireland. She is available for hire on various freelance projects including short story, poetry, songs, recording, novel, and travel writing.

You can read more about Kinbria, her music, and her writings, and purchase her albums and poetry book online at www.kinbria.com.

She Came to Say Good-bye

by Renie Burghardt
Missouri, United States

I was a child of World War II, having been born in Hungary. My young mother died a couple of weeks after my birth, and my father was away because of the war, so I was raised by my maternal grandparents.

When you're a child of war, you're never sure what the next minute, next hour, or next day may bring. All you can do is hope and pray that it will all soon be over. That's what I did, day after day.

We lived in the Bacska region of Hungary near the Serbian border, so when in the spring of 1944, Tito's communist partisans were closing in, many Hungarians decided to leave. We were no exception.

Grandfather conferred with his youngest brother, Tamas, and our two families made plans to go to Kalocsa where Great-uncle Peter, my grandfather's oldest brother, lived. I was seven at the time and was happy that we'd be going together since Uncle Tamas' youngest daughter, Anni, was my age and was the closest thing to a sister I would ever have. We had been inseparable all our lives.

The following couple of days were taken up with packing the few things we would be taking along. Most of our belongings were to be left behind. Grandmother agreed that I could take two of my favorite storybooks with me; the rest of my toys and books would be left.

"We can read to each other on the train," I told Anni. Reading was my favorite pastime.

"Yes, and we can watch the scenery. The train will go right by Lake Balaton," Anni said excitedly.

Lake Balaton was Hungary's largest lake. We had learned about it in school but had never seen it, so this was something we looked forward to. Anni and I also looked forward to seeing our cousin, Agi, Uncle Peter's youngest child, whom we hardly knew. She was nine, and in a letter to us she wrote that she couldn't wait to see us.

The night before we were to leave for the train station Grandfather suddenly had an abrupt change of plans because of a feeling he had.

"We are not taking the train. We are going in the wagon instead," he announced.

"But it will take you eight days by wagon. By train you'll be there in three days," said Uncle Tamas.

"I know, I know. But we can pack much more into the wagon and take it along. We have very little money left. Things are expensive. Why leave the few things we still have behind? Besides, I have a bad feeling about the train."

"Well, we are taking the train just as we planned. So we will be seeing you in about six days," was the last thing Uncle Tamas said before he left for home and Anni and I said our sad good-byes.

Of course I was upset by Grandfather's change of plans. It meant that Anni and I would not be traveling together. And it also meant that Anni would get to Agi's house long before I did. But I knew that once Grandfather made up his mind about something, there would be no changing it, whether I liked it or not.

All that night my grandparents worked on packing things into that horse-drawn wagon. Then early the following morning, while the guns of the partisans could be heard in the distant hills, we boarded the wagon and left the village of our birth for good.

Once the wagon was on the road, and I was comfortably snuggled into my featherbed in the back of the wagon, the journey got more interesting. There were hundreds of people on the road with their wagons, all of them in hopes of finding safety somewhere in our country. When we heard warplanes approaching, we'd all scramble out of our wagons and run and lie down in a ditch, just in case those silver cigars above us would decide to drop some bombs on us.

At night we camped together somewhere along the road, and the men built little fires so the women could cook their meager suppers. And again, if news was heard that warplanes were heading our way, people rushed to put out the fires and ran for ditches or the nearby woods with prayers on their breath!

On the sixth day of our journey we reached Lake Balaton. I gazed at the shimmering waters and thought of Anni, and how she and Agi must already be having fun together. There were beautiful villas along the lake, too, and I wondered if the people living in them felt safer in their placid lake homes.

We found a public area of the lake and took the horses for a drink, while we washed our hands and faces for the first time in days. Then we settled down to spend the night there, before joining the line of wagons again in the morning.

As I lay on my featherbed in the wagon I could see the moonlight casting silver beams on the waters of the lake. It was such a beautiful, tranquil setting that I forgot all about the dangers and hardships of war. Suddenly, I heard a voice calling my name and I sat up and saw her. It was Anni, smiling and waving at me from the edge of the lake, her entire being shimmering, too, as if she was an angel. She looked so happy and beautiful!

"Anni, you're here! I thought you were in Kalocsa already," I called back to her happily. At that point, my grandmother, who was asleep next to me, woke up, and sat up too.

"Anni is out there by the lake," I said. "I just saw her. She was waving to me."

"I don't see anything," Grandma said. "You must have been dreaming. But you will see Anni in two days, sweetheart. Go back to sleep now."

I looked to the area where I had seen Anni standing, but she was no longer there, so I decided that Grandma was right, it must have been a dream. I fell asleep, remembering Anni's smiling, shimmering face, happy that we'd be together soon. And the following morning we were on the road again before the sun came up.

Finally, after what seemed like an eternity to a seven-year-old, we arrived in the city of Kalocsa, and soon pulled into Uncle Peter's property. Uncle Peter and Aunt Roszi came running out of the house to greet us, followed by cousin Agi.

"Where are Tamas and his family?" I heard Grandfather ask, as I was getting ready to jump to the ground.

"You mean you haven't heard?" Uncle Peter asked, his expression turning grave.

"Heard what?"

"The train they were traveling on got hit by bombs. Everyone on that train was killed. Blown beyond recognition. It was on the radio. I thought you knew by now."

I'll never forget my grandfather's reaction upon hearing the news that his "baby" brother was gone. He buried his face in his hands and sobbed uncontrollably. It was the first time I had seen him cry.

"I told him I had a bad feeling about taking the train. But he wouldn't listen," Grandfather kept saying over and over, while Grandmother held me close and tried her best to comfort me, for I was crying, too.

But there was no comfort in anything anyone did or said, as far as I was concerned. Anni was gone. But why, why did it have to happen to Anni? I kept asking my grandmother.

"Only God knows the answer to that, sweetheart," Grandma answered solemnly.

Grandma took me in her arms that evening, and once again tried to console me.

"Remember the dream you had of Anni at the lake?" she asked gently.

"Oh yes, I remember," I sobbed.

"Well, I was wrong. I don't think it was a dream, after all. Anni came to say good-bye to you. She wanted you to know that she was all right and happy. Remember, she is an angel now, but she wanted to say good-bye to you, because she loved you."

And Grandma's words did console me, for I realized she was right. Anni had come to say good-bye to me.

I don't know why Anni and her family perished at that time, while we made it, but I will never forget Anni's shimmering face at the lake and knowing that she was happy on the other side.

Renie Burghardt, who was born in Hungary, is a freelance writer with numerous credits in magazines, books, and online venues. She has been a contributing writer to *Chicken Soup for the Horse Lover's Soul*, *Chicken Soup for the Christian Family Soul*, over a dozen *Guideposts* books, three *Cup of Comfort* books, several *Chocolate for Women* books, *God's Way for Women*, the first *Haunted Encounters*, and many others. She lives in Ozark country, and loves nature, animals, gardening, reading, boating on the river, and spending time with her family and friends.

All Saints' Cottage

by Morag McIntyre Hadley
Bristol, Great Britain

I'd never believed in ghosts — that is, until we bought a sixteenth-century thatched cottage. It was situated in an idyllic country village near Cambridge, England. There was a large garden with an orchard and pond. A stile gave access to a path across the melds to the ancient parish church and to walks through the beautiful countryside — all that we'd ever wanted. There were even roses round the door.

Inside were original doors and skull-cracking beams in every room. Stone flagged floors and mullioned windows completed the period atmosphere. Mike, my husband, loved it from the moment we moved into it. Being used to our previous house with its high ceilings and windows, I found the cottage dark and claustrophobic.

Toward the end of our first summer there an odd thing happened. I was in the garden picking blackberries. I felt a tugging at my skirt and brushed away what I thought was a briar. It happened again. I repeated my action and went on filling my bowl with luscious berries. Another tug; stronger this time. I yelled at our contrary dog, telling him to stop it, thinking that he was probably bored, wanting his afternoon walk and pulling at my skirt. I looked over my shoulder. The dog was asleep under the shade of an ancient plum tree.

I went back to my fruit picking. A few moments later there was another sharp tug, insistent this time. There was nothing to see; there was no one there. A cool breeze sprang up from nowhere and I retreated indoors.

That autumn and winter, Mike was away on extended business trips. I was a bit lonely, particularly during the evenings. I tried to relax with a good book in front of the log fire. This proved to be impossible.

Each evening, usually around nine o'clock, the dog became uneasy. His hackles rose; he looked toward the old, latched door, then lowered his ears. Sometimes, he gave a little growl. When it first happened, I thought someone had knocked on the front door and I hadn't heard. When I checked, there was no one there. Sometimes the door burst open of its own accord and the dog became quite perturbed, wide-eyed, his whole body stiffening.

The cozy room became icy cold for minutes. It was strange, a bit creepy, but nothing more.

I wasn't afraid — at least not too much, but was glad when Mike returned home.

Our son, Doug, came to stay for a few weeks. This was his first visit to the cottage.

He came to breakfast earlier than usual one morning, looking a bit green round the gills.

"I levitated last night," he told us. I asked him what he meant, and he said that sometime in the middle of the night, he woke to find himself floating about two feet above his bed. I hadn't told him about the tugging at my skirt and of the dog's unease on those nights when Mike was away.

During the time we lived in the cottage, pragmatic Mike experienced nothing that was unusual. He put the dog's behavior down to his eccentricity (he was a bit daft), mine to an overactive imagination, and Doug's "levitation" to calling in at the village pub on the way home. Mike continued to love the house, while I felt unsettled and ill at ease.

My mother died that year. Mike was in India on business and Doug had gone back to Sussex and a new job. I was feeling a bit low and missing them. I decided to make myself busy and whitewash the inside of the cottage. It was a wonderful, sparkling winter morning. The windows were open to disperse the smell of paint. My arms and hands were cold as I painted the eaves in our bedroom. I was thinking of my mother and how she loved to paint and wallpaper the house. The memory was a good one and gave me a surge of pleasure.

Then I felt it. Something that felt — because there was nothing to see — like a warm, chubby hand emerging from the sloping eaves and grasping my arm. A spread of comforting warmth radiated from my wrist upward, then coursed through my body. The frosted sun shimmered and, for a moment, I was somewhere else. I didn't know where and I still don't know. It was as if time stood still. When I came to, I experienced a wonderful feeling of tranquility.

I told no one about this except Mike. He suggested that, possibly, it was part of the grieving process for my Mum — my way of coping — or that I'd got pins and needles in my arm. But it hadn't been that. I was certain.

The dog and I never did settle into that idyllic cottage. Just before we left I learned that, toward the end of the nineteenth century, the house had belonged to the church and had been used as an orphanage for children from London. An early photograph from the parish records showed little boys in knickerbockers and little girls with pinafores covering dingy dresses standing in front of the cottage. There were accounts in the annals of the parish of the hilarity of the children when their beds sometimes fell through rotting rafters to the floor below. It was reported in the parish records that All Saints' cottage was cold and damp.

Another photograph showed the children working at their own little garden plots — near the orchard where I'd been picking blackberries. Their mischievous faces twinkled at me from the grainy photograph. I imagined them sneaking in through the old latched door during those dark winter evenings, to cluster round my feet, enjoying the warmth from the log fire, and I was glad. I hoped it was so.

There was no record, either written or verbal, of the cottage being haunted. There was no explanation for the invisible handclasp from the eaves or my son's levitation.

I felt relief at leaving, but sad because I had to leave the "children" behind.

Morag Hadley is Scottish, now living in England. She worked and lived in Bangkok and Singapore for some years. She started writing when she retired from the British Council and has had short stories published in various anthologies and radio, and received awards for short stories, drama, and poetry. This is the first factual experience she has written about, but draws on her life experiences for ideas for fiction. Morag has a Masters degree in Creative Writing. She believes that her awareness was inherited from her Scottish grandmother and half-Irish mother who were able to see the "wee folk" (fairies) and which enabled her to have the experience she writes about here. Writing and reading give her great pleasure, and she also enjoys travelling very much, Canada and America in particular.

Holidays are spent walking (sometimes scrambling) up mountains. Her most fantastic holiday was spent in India, visiting Kashmir and Kadakh and viewing the Himalayas.

The Doctor's House

by Michael Cole
Ontario, Canada

My tale begins, as so many often do, with childhood memories of a strange old house in the country. I was very young when my family moved from the relatively large city of London, Ontario, a few hours northeast to a sleepy village in the country. The term "village" itself is even generous, for the hamlet of Churchill in the mid-70s consisted largely of a rural crossroads clustered with a general store, a church, and a few odd houses. Only the fact that it lay upon a well-traveled highway saved it from complete anonymity.

The house itself was old, even then. Its weathered red bricks had already seen close to a hundred winters. Character emanated from its every beam and window, indices to a colorful history. The building stood on the southeast corner of the busy rural crossroads, enjoying a commanding view of the surrounding countryside in all directions. With the full third-story attic and pointed gables, the house stood tall, and yet its flaking eaves were nonetheless dwarfed by the two massive willow trees that flanked the northern boundary of the property, a tentacled buffer between house and road. Their cascading branches swept out over the lawn to the edge of the road. Farther along in line, there were remnants of a third mighty tree in the decaying girth of a broad stump that jutted only a foot or so above the unkempt tangle of grass and weeds.

The house was quite large, much larger than our needs, but the price and location were to my parents' liking. We had been told that previous to the recent spate of short-term tenants, the home had once belonged to the only doctor in the area. Decades before, when there was no medical facility within safe distance, the doctor's home had doubled as the local hospital. Many of the rooms in the house had therefore served some sort of medical purpose during the doctor's many years in residence.

The interior was both spacious and strange, owing both to its era of construction and its former purpose. High ceilings and hardwood floors meant that sound echoed well throughout the house, including every creak and groan of its aging timbers. A large room at the back of the home was actually a converted gymnasium, complete with basketball nets and court lines on the floor. I still recall the ominous rumble of my tricycle grinding relentless circles on the wooden surface.

The sense of space in the house was creepy, foreboding. As a child, I never wanted to be caught more than one room away from another living soul. Occasionally, play would get the better of me and I would lose track, suddenly realizing that I had strayed too far, only to rush frantically through the void of empty rooms until I found somebody.

By far the creepiest place in the house was the old cellar, a cold, dark dirt basement. We seldom ventured down there, as it was too damp and musty to store anything of value within. The cellar had been useful, however, in the past, as evidenced by the chains and manacles that hung upon two of the rough stone walls. Apparently, in the doctor's day, the state of medicine was such that certain mental disorders were not well understood. Patients that were deemed temporarily insane, even as a result of what we would now characterize as a seizure, would be taken to the cellar and chained to the wall. Here they could be restrained, to exhaust their illness without physical harm to themselves or others.

Few were the times I had the nerve to go to the basement, even in the company of others, and to this day I shudder to think of the "primitive care" that may have transpired in days gone by in the hard, damp earth below our house.

But I have spoken only of my days in the old house. Though its walls and halls were eerie by day, they became quite disturbing by night. Strange things would happen in the night, and I can only be thankful that my tender age at the time protected me from a full realization of events.

Near the top of the stairs to the second floor there was a half-door in the wall, which led to the stairs up to the attic. Every night when we went to bed, one of my parents would check the bolt on the half-door to ensure that it was fully closed. Despite this precaution, every single morning we awoke to find the half-door ajar. Not only was the door unbolted, but standing slightly open, with a chilly breeze wafting down from the attic and out into the staircase. Short of eventually nailing the door shut, this continued to occur on a daily basis.

As strange as this may seem on its own, there were other oddities in the night. Lying awake in my bed, there were times that I could swear I heard those chains in the basement rattling, the metallic clinking echoing through the silence of the house. Moreover, I was not alone in hearing the chains, for my sister, two years older than I, also vividly remembers the eerie rattling of chains. The links reverberated as if thrashed violently by angry captives, seeking to break their shackles and win their freedom from the damp cellar. It is likely that more than one mentally ill patient imprisoned below found freedom from the chains through death.

My sister is alone in one memory she retains of the house. The room that she inherited had apparently been the former nursery in the time of the doctor. It was here that newborn babies were cared for, and likely in those days, it was here that a few of those babies may have died. The doctor would have been by necessity a specialist of all branches of medicine, and yet during a difficult childbirth could likely do no more for a sickly newborn than a midwife. My sister always swore back then that she could hear babies crying in her room, and that they would not let her sleep with their constant wailing. None of the rest of us ever heard a sound.

But the most eerie occurrence in the house happened one time only. Late one Saturday night, the entire family was in bed, sleeping. The four of us were torn from slumber by the sounds of a horrific crash. The noise was deafening, sounding like it was happening just outside our house — a symphony of shattering glass, squealing tires, shrieking metal, and the screams of the dying. In our own rooms, we each ran to our windows to look out onto the road. There was nothing.

The whole family hurried downstairs and huddled onto the porch in the stillness of the night. My father actually got into the car and drove up and down the four directions of the crossroads, so certain was he that a terrible accident had happened and that people needed help. The roads were quiet, with not a soul out traveling this late at night.

Eventually, we all went back to bed, to what few hours of fitful rest remained. If all four of us had not heard the same thing, independently in our own rooms, it might not have seemed so real. The next morning, my father was across the corner at the general store, talking to the owner. He was an elderly gentleman and had spent most of his life in the area. After some hesitation, my father described our experience from the night before.

The old man was silent for a moment, and then explained that there had been a horrible car accident many years ago, when the doctor still lived and practiced in the house. On that exact date, a carful of people were coming home from a party late at night. Nobody knows how heavily the driver had been drinking, but they lost control of the vehicle as they approached the crossroads. The car swerved off the road and onto the doctor's lawn, slamming full force into the third willow tree in line.

Awakened by the crash, the doctor had run out and administered what help he could, but in vain. All four of the passengers had died on his lawn, the spot marked still by the rotting stump of the willow tree. The tree had to be cut down following the tragedy.

The doctor had passed away years later. For our part, we did not live in the house very long, not quite a full year. The house still stands today, a red-brick sentinel of the crossroads, though all else around it has grown up. Many more houses now crowd along the busy roads, flanked by trees both old and new. There is a new owner at the general store, and I see a new family living in my old house as I sit across the road in my car. The new owners of the house also have children, a little older than I was when I lived there almost thirty years ago. They are playing outside, driving trucks and serving tea on the natural tabletop afforded by the old stump on the corner of the lawn.

By day, Michael Cole is an agricultural inspector for the Canadian government in Barrie, Ontario. By night, he enjoys martial arts and a second career in freelance writing. Mike offers various creative and technical writing services through his personal business, Writer's Kramp. His recent works include several technical manuals, a variety of professional correspondence, and personalized family biographies for interested clients. In addition, Mike is currently collaborating on a travel book with Jane Cox of Echoes in Tyme Creative Photography, and is also working on a novel set in a rugged Newfoundland outport. He can be contacted at writerskramp@hotmail.com.

E-Ghost: Electronic Links to the Other Side

by Lawrence Robinson
California, United States

The screen crackled and fizzled. I clicked "New Mail" and an icy chill danced down my spine. It was the same feeling that swept over me when I woke up in the middle of the night to the sound of a creaking door or a bump on the roof or the eerie tapping of rain on the window: a sudden, almost paralyzing sense of foreboding. There was another one of the messages in my inbox — another email with a return path to my own address.

I opened it. The message read: "something's very wrong something's very wrong" repeated, like all the others, for a dozen lines without spacing. "Pain help me," the last one read, "you are fried," the one before it. The messages were at the same time meaningless yet vaguely threatening.

I checked the date on the email. Sent at 11:20 P.M., July 3, 2002, Pacific Daylight Time. Nothing unusual about that. Except that today's date was June 29. If that wasn't unsettling enough, I caught sight of the phone line and network cable dangling like lifeless fingers over the edge of the desk. The PC wasn't even connected to the net.

I left my apartment and ran through the night to a 24-hour cyber cafe on the outskirts of Hollywood. Determined not to end up as fodder for an urban legend or some online X-file, I spent the night in the coffee shop surfing the net, trying to find an explanation, preferably one that didn't involve the supernatural or the possibility that I was losing my mind.

The first thing I discovered was less than reassuring. For more than fifty years people have reported receiving messages, voices, and apparitions through electronic devices such as television, radio, and the telephone. According to Instrumental Transcommunication (ITC) researchers — the Agent Mulder of mysticism investigation — even such a rational and precise calculating machine as a computer is not immune to paranormal weirdness. Instead of consulting a gypsy psychic or Ouija board to contact the poor departed, we should simply flick on a PC. Even spooks and spirits have entered the electronic age.

Electronic voice phenomena (EVP) enthusiasts have long used ordinary tape recorders in quiet secluded areas — such as cemeteries at night — to capture "voices of the dead" that are only audible when the tape is played back at high volume. The International Ghost Hunters Society (http://photos2.ghostweb.com/evp.html) has a number of creepy audio files it claims were recorded this way.

In 1990 ITC pioneer George W. Meek lost his wife to a long illness. Three months after her funeral he claims he received a letter from her via a computer in his Luxembourg research facility. To support the validity of her ITC contact, the spirit of Mrs. Meek highlighted three private events known only to her, her husband, and their secretary, Molly:

> *Dear G.W.*
>
> *Well, it seems there are still people who do not believe in the contacts your friends here in Luxembourg are having. Hence I will give you some personal details known only to you and Molly.*

First story. In 1987, end of April, our tenant Debbie called to say her refrigerator was off. It must have been on a Thursday morning...

Second story. On April 29, 1987, Ann Valentin wrote a letter from California saying she had not received the Magic of Living Forever booklets she had ordered, but instead had received a box of Harlequin novels.

Third story. John Lathrop shut off the electricity at our rental house to put in the new yard light, he wasn't down there very long but charged $20 service in addition to $40 for the bulbs, plus tax. The charge seemed high.

Don't try to explain this, honey, my never-ending love to you. I miss you so much, but I know we will be together...

Love forever,

Jeannette Duncan Meek

According to George Meek, the second item about romance novels was a complete puzzle even to him. When he contacted Ann Valentin in California, however, she confirmed that a carton of novels had indeed arrived mysteriously in 1987, and she still had no idea who'd sent them.

For those who want to believe in all things paranormal, cyberspace has the potential to bridge the chasm between the physical and the spiritual worlds.

But there is usually also a scientific explanation to most "supernatural" phenomena; there is always the logical voice of an Agent Scully. With regard to EVP recordings, there's an obvious possibility of hoaxing or of accidentally recording distant human voices or wayward radio signals. With a networked computer, mysterious messages could originate from anywhere. This could even be true for computers that aren't connected to networks or phone lines.

"Van Eck phreaking" is a form of eavesdropping in which special equipment is used to pick up the electromagnetic (EM) fields that are produced by computer signals, thus allowing a third party access to my computer screen. This electromagnetic radiation is present in computer displays that use cathode ray tubes (CRTs) as well as printers and other devices. Depending on the type of CRT used, the sensitivity of the detection equipment, and the general level of EM energy in the area, Van Eck phreaking can be performed over distances of several hundred feet.

Using a sufficiently powerful transmitter, Van Eck phreaking can make it possible for a message to appear on someone's computer from a remote distance. This would certainly help explain the appearance of the "something's very wrong something's very wrong" emails on my non-networked PC.

Apparently, accomplished hackers are even able to manipulate this effect to get the computer to execute other programs remotely, such as activating a printer or scanner. Even if such mischief wasn't being conducted deliberately, there is always the possibility that a computer is receiving misrouted network email or random Van Eck signals purely by accident.

This rational explanation, coupled with the first rays of morning sunlight creeping into the coffee shop, reassured me and I prepared to return to my apartment. But there was still a distant, nagging doubt in the back of my mind that there may be a third explanation lurking in the shadows, one that falls somewhere between the rational and the supernatural. Call it the "cigarette-smoking man" if you like. I recalled the words of Albert Einstein: "something deeply hidden has to be behind things."

In the 1930s Harold Saxton Burr, a professor at Yale School of Medicine, began researching the role of electricity in living things and concluded, "there is unequivocal evidence that wherever there is life, there are electrical properties." He contended that man, and indeed all life forms, are ordered and controlled by electrodynamic fields. In other words, life and the human body, much like a computer, is to a large extent electromagnetic in nature.

Therefore, it is possible that a life form exists that is entirely electromagnetic. If such a life form does exist and it wanted to contact humans, the obvious channel would be through electromagnetic equipment — a home computer, for example.

Exhausted, I called a halt to my investigation at this point. Later that morning, I traded in my PC and changed my Internet service provider and the mysterious emails stopped. Whichever explanation you're inclined to believe, the truth is out there, somewhere in cyberspace. Or else something's very wrong.

Lawrence Robinson is a journalist and author based in Los Angeles. His work has appeared in publications such as *Arena*, *The Face*, *Icon*, *Loaded*, and *LA Weekly*.

The Lady on the Verandah

by Ann Howard
Sydney, Austraila

When my mother and father split up, my mother took us to live in a big old rambling house on an island set on the mighty Hawkesbury River, two hours north of Sydney, Australia. My mother, my two younger brothers, and I settled in with our few possessions and started to make our home there.

My mother had wanted to write for a long time and my father had gotten tired of making her go to business dinners and functions and looking at her stony expression, so he finally agreed to stay in Sydney. They weren't divorced, just separated and he visited every couple of weeks.

It was a real adventure for us kids. The house was built in 1874, really old for Australia. It was in a ramshackle state with rosellas flashing their jewel-like colours as they flew through the large main room where creepers hung through broken window-panes. In England, where we came from originally, the authorities would not have let us live in such a place. There was an inside toilet but no bath and the roof leaked in several places. Here, in a subtropical zone, it didn't matter. Apart from the mosquitoes flying in at night, what were a few broken panes of glass to worry about? It was always warm and the rain was clean and sweet.

Every time my father came, something got fixed. The roof was mended, a bath put in, the glass replaced. The house was full of furniture from the old days, all in a state of disrepair. While my mother thought about her writing, she worked on cleaning and restoring the big cedar table, the chairs, and the marble washstand. Gradually we had a home to be proud of.

The biggest work was in the garden. Neglected wasn't the word. We wanted to swim and fish in the river but we made an agreement with my mother that we would work in the garden every afternoon for two hours. The little ones often ran off with their friends, but they could not do much heavy work anyway. So it was usually my mother and me clearing fallen branches, raking, and cutting back lantana and roses.

Along the river side of the old house was a verandah. One afternoon we were in the north corner of the garden. I was tying up grape vines, and my mother was weeding a path. She straightened up and stretched her back, looking toward the verandah. I heard her intake of breath as she pointed.

"I can see a woman in a long white dress, walking toward the verandah rail," she said with a low, soft voice.

I was fourteen, strong enough to pull the boat in by myself, but I was terrified. I could not see what my mother was pointing at, but I had never heard her speak in that tone of voice before. There was a still, cold darkness in our part of the garden.

"Don't, don't!" I yelled, dropping the twine and pushing my mother to one side. To my shame, I ran up the little lane at the side of the house, my heels hardly touching the ground.

Later at supper, she said mildly, "Ann, I don't know why you were so frightened back there. I think it was a ghost I saw, but why do we have to be frightened of ghosts?"

Two years went by. The house was now unrecognizable. The antique furniture glowed and smelled of beeswax. The linen cupboard was sweet with lavender. The glass was replaced, the coloured glass sparkling. Mother had made friends and she was happy and smiling. Most importantly, she had her first book published.

She joined a historical society. One afternoon, she came back very excited.

"I've found a lady, aged eighty-three, in a retirement home, who used to visit this house as a child. Her father took many photographs in the old days and she's going to bring some for us to see."

Mrs. Osborne was very gracious about the work we had done on the house. In the old days she had to be segregated from her brother in the swimming pool at the early age of seven. They had to bathe fully dressed. Mother had made a Pavlova and taken out her best china tea set.

"Here is the album I promised you," Mrs. Osborne said.

Mother opened the album somewhere near the centre. She gave a cry.

"There's the woman! The woman in white! This is the woman I saw on the verandah. Do you remember, Ann?"

I looked nervously at the black and white photo. It was slightly fuzzy but you could quite clearly see a young woman with a tiny waist, her hair swept up about her oval face. She was wearing a white dress with a long train. She was resting her hand on the verandah rail as though looking toward the river for something.

"Who was she?" my mother asked Mrs. Osborne.

"My cousin, Albertine."

"Was she happy here? Did something happen to her?"

"As far as I know, she was very happy here. She came often in the summer. She met a handsome naval officer who used to come and take her out for picnics. This photo is of her watching for him to sail to the jetty."

"She is here because she was so happy here and she wants us to be happy too," murmured my mother.

A few months later, my father rang up and said that he was now able to work part time from home and that he was going to come and live with us again. Mother was very happy with this. She had her own study and could write in the mornings. She hugged us all.

That afternoon, I was coming back from the river and I stopped in the north corner of the garden. Something made me look up at the verandah. She floated into view. Her face was indistinct, but I could see the tiny waist and the fall of her white dress. Her hand rose and fluttered as if in greeting, or was it good-bye? Nobody ever saw her again but Albertine's roses over that part of the verandah were the sweetest for miles around.

Ann Howard is a grandmother who was born in England but lives in Australia. As you can see from her picture, she enjoys life but assures the reader that her ghost story is absolutely true. She still lives in that house and has the picture of the lady whose ghostly figure appeared to her and her mother on her wall. Ann is a frequently published fiction and historical nonfiction writer.

Brad's Story

by Laurie Moore
Texas, United States

As an attorney with a general practice that includes an occasional divorce, I'm well aware that even though a husband or wife can be replaced — I see it done with alarming regularity — whether it's wanted or not, the effect of ending a marriage is still comparable to a death in the family. If you accept this premise as truth, then you must also accept another.

You can never replace a child.

While Grant was my nephew, I felt the sting of his death almost as much as my sister. When he was a baby, I had been one of his caretakers, and I grew to love him as if he were my own.

His unexpected death rocked my family, but questioning the Christian teachings I had been raised on as a child resulted in the deepest fissures. Outwardly, I appeared to be fine. Inwardly, I was a mess. My belief system had crumbled, and no one had been able to restore my faith.

Three months after Grant's death, I took an externship with the District Attorney's Office. While learning the ins and outs of prosecutorial intake, I made a new friend.

My gravitation to Glenda was instant. She had an easy way about her, as well as an inherent sense of deep wisdom. It didn't hurt that we shared a common bond. She was a police officer on loan to the DA; prior to getting my law degree, I had been a police officer with a different department.

Rather than live with the institutional colors of a government building, Glenda transformed her office into an oasis of beauty. Prints of paintings by post-impressionist artists hung on her walls, their colors soothing to the eye. But the most notable work of art in the room was the photograph she displayed on her desk: the charming picture of a little boy dressed in coveralls, wearing a train engineer's cap. The child's eyes held an unmistakable twinkle; his winning smile beamed remarkable.

Glenda caught me staring.

"That's my son Brad."

"He's precious."

Without warning, her eyes misted. "He kept that hat on all the time." She mustered a stoic smile. "He lost his hair. See… Brad died of leukemia."

I felt the lump in my throat harden. If anyone could help me understand how to deal with the void in my heart, I knew Glenda could. I pushed the door shut, and eased into a chair across the desk.

Words spilled out.

Then came the tears.

When I finished Grant's story, I confessed that his sudden death had devastated my faith. Glenda nodded knowingly and spoke of her son.

Once Brad's doctors diagnosed him with leukemia, he experienced periods of moderate improvement in his struggle to beat the disease, followed by downturns that left Glenda and her husband frantic with worry. She made sure Brad took the prescribed medication, explaining in simple terms meant for a child that he needed it in order to get well.

In time, Brad's condition deteriorated. His hair fell out and Glenda knew it was only a matter of time before he would end up back in the hospital. Heartsick, she tried to prepare her child for death.

"He was so tiny to have such tragic circumstances heaped on him, but he had such keen insight for his age. I realized he wouldn't improve, and I didn't want him to be afraid."

Trinity Park is a place of beauty. It covers an area west of downtown Fort Worth where the Trinity River winds past like a shimmering serpent between the banks below. To help ease the pain, Glenda took Brad on a ride to see "his trees." During this drive, she broke the news: the medicine wasn't working. He wouldn't get better.

"One day the angels will come and take you."

Brad said, "They've already come."

In her astonishment, Glenda thought she misheard him. "What?"

"They've already come and I told them no."

Several times, he spoke of seeing "the light."

When Brad returned to the hospital the next day, Glenda confided in his doctor. "Whatever meds you have him on are making him hallucinate. He says he's seeing lights."

The doctor regarded her with compassion. His words came out gentle and resigned. "No, he really does see the light."

Glenda kept a vigil in Brad's room. Friends hearing the sad news flocked to see her. One in particular encouraged her to take a break. To leave the hospital for a quick bite to eat, so she could return to Brad's bedside refreshed.

"How can I leave my child, knowing he might die while I'm gone?"

The friend brought back food.

Glenda and her husband notified relatives. Anyone wanting to see Brad needed to come right away.

Family members arrived to say their good-byes. During the night, Brad fell into a coma-like sleep.

The next day, in the early afternoon, those who gathered with Glenda and her husband left the room. It wouldn't be long; the parents needed privacy with their baby. Through their intense grief, Glenda and her husband stayed by their son's side, watching his life ebb away.

Without warning, Brad opened his eyes.

He spoke with great clarity. "The angels are here."

Glenda surrendered her will. "It's okay to go."

Glenda watched her baby's eyes close. It was as if she had given him permission.

Then, he was gone.

"The minute he shut his eyes, you could feel it — such an incredible sensation that filled the entire room."

I knew the pain she relived as she told Brad's story. To say it helped reaffirm the teachings of childhood would minimize the impact this shared moment had on me. I knew, the way Brad had known, that Grant was in a better place; and it cemented my belief in the hereafter.

Glenda retired from the PD and took a position at an elementary school. She recently shared her tragedy with the school counselor. Together, they started a fundraiser called "Pennies for Leukemia" to raise awareness of the killer disease. A newsletter highlighted the event, and Glenda was invited to speak to the elementary students about Brad's courageous struggle.

Schoolchildren were asked to donate their pennies to help other children like Brad.

"We calculated that if all the children were moved to donate their extra pennies, our efforts might raise as much as three or four hundred dollars to fund leukemia research."

They had no idea Brad's story would bring in over six thousand dollars.

I asked Glenda if I could share Brad's story.

"If it's helpful... if it can ease another's suffering... then, do it."

Laurie Moore, Edgar-nominated author of *Constable's Apprehension*, was born and reared in the Great State of Texas. She's traveled to forty-nine U.S. states, most of the Canadian provinces, Mexico, and Spain. She received her Bachelor of Arts degree in Spanish, English, and Elementary and Secondary Education from the University of Texas at Austin. Instead of using her teaching certificate, she entered into a career in law enforcement, ranging from patrol work to District Attorney investigator. She received her Juris Doctor from Fort Worth's Texas Wesleyan University School of Law in 1995. She is currently in private practice in "Cowtown," and has a daughter at Rhodes, a destructive Siamese cat, and a sneaky Welsh corgi. She is still a licensed, commissioned peace officer. Laurie is a member of the DFW Writer's Workshop and an office holder on the DFWWW Board of Directors. She is the author of four published novels: *Constable's Run*, *The Lady Godiva Murder*, *Constable's Apprehension*, and *The Wild Orchid Society*; and several short stories in *Haunted Encounters* and *Heroes for Humanity*. Writing is her passion. Contact Laurie through her web site at www.LaurieMooreMysteries.com.

Pen-y-Bryn

by Jany Gräf-Hessing
Caan, Germany

It's been a long time since I left Newport. In those days, back in the '50s, it was a small town in the backwaters of Shropshire, one of the heartland counties of England. My parents and I moved away in 1956 — they told me later it was because my dad had to find a new job. But he'd only just started at a local business and was running the export department single-handedly, much to the delight of his bosses, who were impressed by his foreign language skills. I'd just started school and was doing really well. No, there must have been some other reason for the hasty uprooting of our household.

It must have been because of what happened in that house. Looking back, I often wonder why my parents didn't sense there was something wrong when they first set eyes on the place. Don't they always say that violent, traumatic events leave behind an aura that stays with a house forever?

It happened in a sprawling Georgian mansion called "Pen-y-Bryn," which is Welsh for "the brow of the hill," as harmless a name as a house ever had. A large, 21-room place surrounded by sweeping lawns and high hedges, it was as near to Manderley as a little girl might imagine. In those early days we didn't have many possessions to furnish such a large home, and we spent most of the time huddled together in the kitchen — it was the only room small enough to heat effectively. The vast fireplaces in the empty morning room and the drawing room would have devoured a tree trunk each, but our budget only ran to a few scoops of coal.

The many larders and pantries stood deserted, as did the nursery and the nanny's quarters. The gigantic, freezing-cold bathroom upstairs, painted from floor to ceiling in pale pink, right down to the bathtub, window frames, and door handles, never heard a child splashing in it. The sickly sweet paintwork had obviously been someone's cosmetic attempt at making the room seem warm. They needn't have bothered. We had our tin bath in front of the kitchen stove.

Next to my bedroom, with its dark corners full of nameless things, lay the magnificent master bedroom, which my parents used. Their iron-framed double bed stood forlorn at the far-off end. The built-in wardrobes with flaking, cream-painted doors stretched along a whole wall, like a row of parallel rooms. Would my parents have slept so soundly if they'd known that, close by, in the wall at the end of the landing, just outside their room, was a bricked-up door to a disused room? They might never have known if it hadn't been for that summer evening.

They'd tucked me up in bed and gone outside to do some gardening. It was warm and quiet, the sounds of the town muted by the hedges and the big beech tree on the lawn. There was no warning of what was to come.

They say my screams were heart-stopping. Horrified, and fearing some terrible accident, my parents raced into the house and up the long flight of stairs. Panting to the top, and turning right along the landing, they found me standing outside my bedroom door in my nightdress, pointing to the wall at the end of the landing, completely hysterical. With tears streaming down my little face I was pointing to the wall at the end. "There's a man with no legs! Only his top!" I managed to blurt out between sobs. Horrified, they looked round, but could see nothing.

"Well, what does he look like, dear?" my father asked hesitantly.

"He's got a blue coat on with big yellow buttons and… and a big black hat on his head. And he's got a big long stick in his hand!" By now I was trembling all over. "And now he's walking through the wall!" They told me later my eyes were popping out of my head.

Picking me up, my father carried me back to bed, dried my tears, and reassured me that the man wouldn't be coming back.

Puzzled, but assuming I'd just had a nightmare, they went back out into the garden. Most parents would have done the same. Next morning, after taking me to school, my mother stopped to chat with an elderly neighbour. Mrs. Norris lived in the lodge at the entrance to the drive and had known the house in its heyday. After the usual British comments about the weather, Mum, in passing, mentioned the events of the previous evening and my "nightmare." She wasn't prepared for the old lady's reaction.

The woman gaped at her, horrified. "Jany must have seen the coachman!" she whispered. "He always wore a navy blue jacket with gold buttons and a top hat. And he carried a coachman's whip. Oh, there were always rumours about him. He was quite a lad. They say he had an affair with the lady of the house. He'd steal into her bedroom up the back stairs and leave later through the linen room door on the landing. Its other door led to the stairs at the front of the house. Later this room was bricked up on both sides! Didn't you know?"

Shocked, my Mum had to admit she didn't. She was a realistic, down-to-earth woman, but if she'd known before that there was anything supernaturally wrong with Pen-y-Bryn, I doubt whether she'd ever have moved in there.

The subject of the ghostly coachman must have preoccupied my parents for the rest of our stay in Pen-y-Bryn. Strangely enough though, they never questioned me about being out of bed and on the landing that evening. Did they assume I'd been lured out of my bed? As a child you know what to expect when you've done something wrong. My parents were strict and the fact that their little girl had got out of her bed, left her much-loved teddy bear, and wandered through the house would normally not have gone without mention. Maybe they thought the fright I'd had was punishment enough.

Some weeks later, when Dad had to go away for a few days, leaving us alone in the house, they made a point of moving my bed into their bedroom before he left, and Mum left the light on all night. Under the pretext of my feeling safer, of course.

It wasn't long after that we packed up and moved, in fact, we even left the country, settling near my father's family in Holland.

My parents, by nature curious, were strangely enough not too eager to find out more about the history of Pen-y-Bryn. We never discovered why the coachman had appeared to a five-year-old girl on that summer evening. Years later we heard that the house had been demolished. And when the workmen had torn up the floorboards of the morning room, they'd found a baby's skeleton....

Jany Gräf-Hessing is British born and bred (apart from four years in Holland — Dad was a Dutchman, Mum, English). Have had all kinds of jobs — at present part-time tourist-information and museum employee. Place of work: a castle dating from 1850. I'm still looking for the resident ghost! Been writing since I could hold a pencil. I've been published in *Yours* and *Dolls House World*, both U.K. magazines. I love writing humour and nostalgia. Would like to write a regular humorous slot about life in Germany, where I've lived for the last thirty-odd years — and odd they've certainly been. When not occupied with ghostly houses, I like to make dollhouses in 1/12 scale. Other hobbies? Well, painting and drawing, pen pal, gardening, reading, and embroidery, but they all seem to take second place these days after writing (as does housework). I'll drop anything for the Ultimate Granddaughter, Angelina, though. Would love to hear from the like-minded and all the others out there struggling to keep up with J.K. Rowling. I forgot to say I'm a Harry Potter fan too.

Magdalena's Mist

by Kira Connally
Texas, United States

While attending the Spring Spirit Seekers 2003 Paranormal Symposium in Schulenburg, Texas, I was part of a late-night ghost hunt that ended up being scarier than I had expected! The conference was held at the Von Minden Hotel on Lyons Street in historic downtown Schulenburg, and the St. Rose of Lima cemetery was just down the road. As part of the conference, two ghost hunts were conducted at this cemetery, partly because the former owners of the Von Minden are buried here and partly because of its proximity to the hotel. I took part in the Saturday night ghost hunt at the very end of the conference. While it was spooky out there, not much happened.

I'm a member of a ghost-hunting group, and as a group we returned to this cemetery after the conference was over, after midnight that same Saturday. There were eight of us that night, but another member, Jeff Ossenkop, and I wandered off by ourselves almost immediately. This cemetery is full of beautiful, ornate Catholic monuments, and many of the headstones are inscribed in German and Czech. The dead of this cemetery went out in style, and as a result, the cemetery is very well maintained, as if it were truly a place for the living to spend long hours visiting. It appeared that the oldest graves were on the back side of the cemetery closest to the Von Minden Hotel; that's where Jeff and I headed.

We were walking between the aisles of cemented-over plots, when suddenly the air developed a chill. It was after midnight, but this is May in South Texas — there's nothing chilly about that. The plot that was nearest to where we were standing when the air got cool held two graves, one much smaller than the other. It was the smaller one that caught our attention. It was obviously old, of a mottled stone, and had noticeable erosion to the inscription. The name on the weather-beaten headstone was Magdalena; she died in 1899 at about forty years of age. The larger stone belonged to her husband, and it was not only larger but of a better quality. Were I a ghost, I might have wanted to draw attention to this, too! But I suppose this was common in 1899, when the world was so much different.

Jeff and I walked around the cemented edge of the plot and, after a moment's deliberation, stepped inside. It really was cooler here, and the air had a thick quality to it, as if we were in the middle of a New England pea-soup fog. I've never seen fog like that in Texas. I don't know where the rest of the group was, but we couldn't hear them, and I know I wasn't aware of them at all.

When we stepped inside, I started to get chills on my legs and arms, and Jeff had a look on his face that I'd never seen before. It was a mixture of wonder and worry. His eyes narrowed as he read Magdalena's name aloud. As soon as the name was out of his mouth, Jeff tilted to the right a little, and I felt a cold draft swoosh by me. Now Jeff is about six foot six inches tall, and when he tilts over, you can't help but notice! He stayed like that for a second, and then his leg jerked. He said he had been grabbed around the ankle and couldn't move right away! I told him about the cold air I felt rush by, and then he was able to straighten up.

We both looked around, and I know that I didn't see anyone else in the cemetery. I thought perhaps the rest of our group had gone across the street to the newer section of the cemetery where the mausoleum was, beyond where we had parked our cars. As soon as Jeff and I stepped out of the border of the burial plot, we both start snapping as many pictures as we could. His camera has a very brilliant flash, and it was illuminating the fog, creating spooky spiral patterns. I was just watching the patterns in the fog when I heard laughter and whirled around. There was nothing behind me, nor to my side. I looked at Jeff but I don't think he heard it and, not wanting to sound like an idiot, I kept my mouth shut.

We walked a few feet away and took some more pictures, and we stood there a few minutes while I scanned through the digital images I had just taken. None of the mist showed up in the photos. The headstones showed up fine, but nothing else. The flash on my camera is fairly weak, so I chalked it up to that. I could have sworn that I had taken a picture with Jeff in it, but that wasn't there either. I decided that I could look more closely when I got home, and we continued on.

We stopped next at a recent grave, the mound of earth still piled atop the ground, and there were bushes growing here that seemed very out of place. That's when I heard the footsteps. I got the impression that this Magdalena was not a nice woman. I tried to ignore the footsteps and watched Jeff take pictures of the conspicuously placed bush. I heard her laugh, and I turned around, and again there was nothing. A minute or two later I heard the footsteps again, but distant, as if they were retreating. I ignored it. I didn't want to turn around and see her, or get grabbed like Jeff did earlier. Some fearless ghost hunter I am!

When Jeff was done taking pictures, we heard another member of our group calling out to us. They were still on the same side of the road as we were, and when we got to them, they said they had never left this side. A Schulenburg police officer had pulled up to see what us ghost hunters were doing, and they had been talking for about ten minutes, as well as calling for Jeff and me. We never heard them, and certainly never saw them or the police cruiser pull up.

Were Jeff and I surrounded in a cloud of Magdalena's mist, obscuring our vision while we stood there and blocking out the sound of our friends? I don't know, but I know I don't want to encounter the laughing, grabbing ghost of Magdalena again after midnight!

Kira Connally lives in Mineral Wells, Texas, and works as an optician. She grew up in a family that could see and hear spirits, and spends her free time searching for ghostly activity with a group of friends in the Fort Worth area. Kira was also a tour guide at the haunted Baker Hotel in Mineral Wells. Her ghostly adventures can be found at www.blueivvy.com, and she can be contacted at kjc@blueivvy.com.

The Haunting Shadow

by Diana Lee
Yamaguchi-ken, Japan

I really don't know what that shadow was — a ghost, a spirit, or just an inexplicable phenomenon — but it's haunted me for years. It's shattered my firm belief in a world of physical reality. It's convinced me that there is such a thing as fate in one's destiny.

I remember it all began with a series of events that occurred in our house many years ago….

"Where are they?" demanded my mother with one hand on her hip. "Did you take them?"

"Take what?" I asked.

"My eyebrow tweezers. They're missing from my dresser drawer."

"I know nothing about them."

"Where could they be then?" she glared at me. "Don't just stand there! Help me find them."

My mother called my younger brother to join in the search. We looked frantically everywhere in the house; even combed every inch of her bedroom, not once, but three times. Still, we came up empty-handed.

Three days later, I heard my mother's screeching voice in her room. "Aha! Here they are! Right where they're supposed to be!"

Lounging in front of the TV, my brother eyed me suspiciously. "You took 'em, didn't ya?"

"No, I didn't." I shook my head.

"You're the only person, besides Mom, who would use 'em," he said.

"I never touched her stuff."

"Then explain how they got back in the drawer."

"How should I know?" Then it hit me. I suddenly felt cold and numb.

"What's the matter?" he peered at me.

Swallowing hard, "Remember… three nights ago?" my voice quivered.

"It was your thirteenth birthday. So?"

"I had a lot to eat," I began slowly. "Well… I got up to use the bathroom in the middle of the night. The small nightlight was on as usual. I was about to wash my hands, then something on the left wall caught my eye… a shadow that wasn't mine!"

"How d'ya know the shadow wasn't yours?"

"Because my shadow was on the wall behind me."

"Hmm…," he raised his eyebrow. "Go on."

"The shadow was of a perfect-looking man," I shuddered as I spoke. "I'll never forget that chiseled profile as long as I live."

"Then?" he turned the TV volume down.

"I tried to remove all the things off the counter that might have cast the shadow. But even after taking everything out of the bathroom, it was still there."

"Was it still there when you switched the main light on?"

"Don't be silly, all shadows disappeared under the bright light."

I moved closer to him and lowered my voice. "When I looked into the large mirror above the washbasin, all I could see was my own face. Then I turned to look at the shadow." Closing my eyes, I remembered the sensation vividly.

A chill ran through my body and my heart started pounding. Then I opened my eyes and said, "A terrible realization seized me — the shadow was looking right back at me through the mirror!"

"What d'ya mean?" He turned the TV off.

"The shadow and my shadow were facing each other," I whispered. He looked at me with a stone face. I continued, "Everyone was sound asleep, so I crept back to bed — but I couldn't fall back to sleep."

"Why didn't ya tell me about it the next day?"

"I wanted to make sure I wasn't dreaming, so I waited until the following night."

"Well?" he was tapping his fingers on the couch. "Was it still there?"

"No. The shadow was gone," I answered.

Shaking his head, he snickered, "A nightmare. That was all."

"That was what I thought until today. How do you explain the strange incident with the tweezers?" I asked.

"What? You think the shadow had som'thin' to do with it?" His eyes narrowed.

"You know we searched the entire house but couldn't find them before. Today, they popped up at the very spot where Mom always put them." I looked him in the eyes. "Who else could've made the tweezers disappear, reappear, and then make me look like the culprit? Only I could have understood the meaning of it."

"Get outta here!" Turning away, he clicked the TV back on. "I'm sick of your stories. I know you took 'em."

I was afraid to tell anyone else about it because I'd be laughed at or called a liar. In the following years, my life continued as normal without any more unusual occurrences. I thought the odd thing was that the shadow appeared without any reason. It wasn't an omen or someone I knew. It appeared and then disappeared, but left me believing in its existence. The whole event made no sense at all.

Then I started to have doubts about my own experience in seeing the shadow. Maybe it was a dream after all and the incident with the eyebrow tweezers had some rational explanation. Perhaps my mother forgot that she misplaced them or that we overlooked the spot in the drawer where they'd been all the time. From then on, I decided to steer clear away from the paranormal realm by not believing in anything that was not based on scientific fact in our physical world. Eventually, I buried the whole event as though it had never happened.

Seven years later, when I was a junior in college, I had a difficult time deciding on a major. I didn't have a clue as to what I wanted to do in life. One day, while browsing in the campus bookstore, I spotted something on the shelf that stopped me dead in my footsteps — a book cover with the exact profile of the shadow! My hands couldn't stop trembling as I picked the book up — a treatise by David Hume on skepticism. The irony of it was too eerie to ignore! Here was this book jumping out at me about doubting one's own empirical experience. The shadow on the book cover was speaking directly to me about my own doubts of its existence! I knew right then and there that this book had decided my fate to major in philosophy.

After many more years had passed, I finally understood the reason why I saw the shadow on the wall. The shadow has been a guide to my destiny. It played a vital role in shaping my life. And it opened my eyes to a world beyond physical reality. More importantly, it fueled my desire to travel abroad in search of wisdom and of my place in the world. Pursuing an unconventional lifestyle, I've drifted from country to country to find that pot of gold at the end of the rainbow. A friend of mine suggested that I start a cram school in Japan. On my thirtieth birthday, he sent me a gift.

As I unwrapped the package, I gasped and my knees nearly buckled. There it was on the ESL book cover — the chiseled profile of the shadow!

Diana Lee has traveled extensively and worked abroad in Cameroon, China, and Japan. She has been running a cram school and working as a freelance writer in Japan. Her writings have appeared in magazines and e-zines. Interested in various forms of writing, she is now working on short stories and a book. Contact her at dleee@hotmail.com.

In the Family

by Cathy Conrad
Nova Scotia, Canada

When we make the five-hour drive to visit and stay at my grandmother's, the evening adult conversation always rolls around to the ghostly incidents we've experienced lately or recountings of past memorable paranormal events. It has been that way on holidays and visits ever since I can remember and probably long before I was born.

There was always something about our family and ghosts. Maybe it was that many in our family were older and their homes were the only houses they'd ever lived in, and had been owned and handed down by their parents. They are close-knit, set in their ways, and extremely helpful folks, even the members of the younger generation, and they, like their vintage homes, are comfortable to be around and welcoming.

Drop-ins are expected, and, when you do, be ready to eat, because someone is always handing you a plate of whatever is available and a drink. It is perhaps for these reasons that spirits seemed to show up more in our close family than others.

Listening to eerie family stories fascinated me when I was young. I was amazed how everyone discussed their encounters so easily, so matter-of-factly, as if this was the norm. But it was the norm for our family and it wasn't long before I was hooked on listening to any and all stories I could get people to tell.

Spooked, but completely enthralled, I would usually lie on my grandmother's living room sofa in the late hours when we visited, while the adults continued chatting into the night around the kitchen table, and I listened as long as I could before drifting to sleep right there on the sofa, covered by one of my grandmother's many hand-knit afghans. Anyway, there was no way I would go upstairs by myself in that old house. Instead, my mother would take me up when the adults were finally heading to bed. Even now, as an adult, I am not comfortable upstairs in my grandmother's house. I'm not so much scared as I am simply spooked, because I feel that anyone who may be haunting those rooms is definitely a friendly spirit, or spirits.

Most members of my very extended family of parents, grandparents, uncles, aunts, and cousins have had at least one type of paranormal encounter or another, and many have had similar types of encounters, but separately.

One unusual happening that we've all witnessed at one time or another is hearing "steps and three knocks" at the door. I found it hard to believe when I was first told of this as a child, but I know now that the knocks are real, and they bring a message. Usually occurring in the evening, someone is heard walking up the steps to the front door. The steps stop and then come three knocks. More than one person has heard this and dogs have barked as they normally would when someone comes to the door. But when the door is opened, no one is there. Rest assured, within weeks, a member of the family or a close friend will die. It happens so often that we have come to expect this "clue" or "heads up" from our friendly messenger.

My first supernatural experience happened when I was ten years old. I was lying in bed in my own room and my parents were arguing, as they often did at the time. I always found their arguments upsetting, as any child would, but this particular night felt different. Worse. It's not that they got physically violent, although I think it had come close a few times, but it was loud and the words were terribly hurtful to each other.

I didn't know whether to lie in bed, hoping that things would settle down rather than continue to get louder and more frightening to listen to, or get up to let someone know I was awake, which could either put an end to the argument for the evening or could trigger something worse. I am telling you, as a child in that situation, it was a difficult and scary decision to make.

I decided I would get up, even though I had an uneasy feeling about going out into the middle of the fighting. As I pushed the covers aside and began to sit up I was met by a strong, warm wind blowing back at me. I knew immediately that it was something "else," because my door and window were closed and the furnace was not on at that time of year.

The wind rushed past me a few seconds, whooshing past my ears and blowing my hair back. It was forceful — not enough to push me down, but just the right strength to make a definite presence of itself and to tell me what I needed to know: "Don't get out of bed right now."

I trusted the feeling that I got and I stayed put. Soon after, the argument subsided and I drifted off to sleep, feeling comforted that "someone" was there for me that night.

Somehow, that wind, or whoever was behind it, not only kept me out of what probably would have been an extremely uncomfortable situation, but it succeeded in letting me know that things would be okay.

I can't explain how or why, but there was a comforting that came with that warm wind, and my feelings changed that night about my parents' situation. Until then, I worried so much about the possibility of them splitting up. I had always kept those concerns to myself, so no one really knew how much it weighed on my young mind. But now I wanted them to split up, because I could suddenly see and understand that it would be the best for everyone.

That's a big piece of information to absorb as a ten-year-old, but I got it and it felt great. A year later, the divorce was final and things felt more settled and happy than they ever had.

To this day, at thirty-eight, I clearly remember that wind, but I have not experienced it since that night, and neither have I been able to figure out who it might have been — perhaps the same person who's been knocking on our doors these many years. Perhaps when my day comes and I pass on, I will have a chance to meet, and thank, whoever it was that helped me that night.

Cathy Conrad was born and raised in Nova Scotia, Canada. She is thirty-nine, married, and has two daughters, eleven and fifteen.

While working part-time for a local real estate appraisal company for twenty years, Cathy also tries to be at home as much as possible with her children. Recently, she has started pursuing her interest in writing and has had several works published thus far, including a bedroom makeover article and photos published in *Girls' Life* magazine, a how-to e-book published by 29 Ways Press, a greeting card poem accepted by Blue Mountain Arts, a how-to article published by *The Dollar Stretcher*, a children's writing contest win promoted by *Flying Girl*, and, of course, her real-life piece in *Haunted Encounters*.

Ghostly Tales from an English RAF Base

by Pearl A. Gardner
West Yorkshire, England

I married an RAF man in 1974 and went to live in married quarters at a North Yorkshire air base. I'd been living in a small mill town, and moving to the countryside was wonderful. It was so green and peaceful, apart from flying days, when the jet provosts were doing circuits and bumps. RAF Linton on Ouse was a training base for jet pilots at that time, but it used to be an active bomber and fighter station during the Second World War.

There were a few spooky tales doing the rounds, but I didn't think much of them. As I didn't believe in ghosts in those days. I scoffed at the rumours that were buzzing around the base. But it seemed the whole camp was supposed to be haunted. The control tower was thought to be inhabited by a friendly ghostly officer, and the radar and radio operators who worked there saw him frequently. A local television station did a short news item about the sightings, and interviewed some of the people who claimed to have witnessed his ghostly apparition. They all sounded convincing. My husband, who worked as a ground radar and radio technician in the building, had little to say on the subject, even when I quizzed him.

We lived in a small terraced house on Grosvenor Square, and I was grateful we hadn't been allocated a house on Half Moon Street. This street is situated to one end of the long runway, and the story I heard was that the street had been bombed during the last war and many people were killed. The people who now lived there told tales that made me shiver. The inhabitants of Half Moon Street often heard strange sounds in the night. I heard stories of loud wailing, moaning, bumps, thumps, and scratching noises, but nothing that couldn't be put down to overactive imaginations and mice, or so I thought.

However, within weeks of moving into my new home, strange things started happening that I found difficult to explain. I'd put something down and when I came to pick it up seconds later it would have moved. Sometimes into a different room! I'd polish the kitchen floor, and minutes later there would be scratch marks on the shiny surface, but no one had been in the room. I blamed my absentmindedness on the objects I misplaced. I blamed the inferior quality of the polish for not covering the scratch marks that *must* have been there previously.

One night, we'd just gone to bed, and I'd turned out the bedside lamp. A few seconds later it came back on with a clicking sound. I switched it off again, not thinking anything of it. The second time it clicked back on, I asked my husband if he was playing tricks on me. He was a bit of a practical joker. He insisted it wasn't him, and I put it down to a loose wire, even though I couldn't find anything wrong with the lamp the next morning. I found all kinds of excuses for the odd things I was experiencing, until something happened that couldn't be explained, and left me feeling more afraid than I'd ever been in my life.

It was a sunny, late summer morning. I'd been enjoying a coffee break between chores with my husband and two of our friends. We'd been chatting about the ghostly stories we'd heard. We laughed at the people who actually believed the spooky tales. Our friends left, and my husband went to do some work in the garden. I went upstairs to the bathroom. I was washing my hands when I heard loud, heavy footsteps climbing the stairs. I immediately thought my husband was playing a joke and trying to scare me, especially given the topic of our recent conversation. I told him that I wasn't afraid. "I know it's you!" I called through the bathroom door. I smiled to myself when the footsteps halted, thinking I had spoiled his fun. When the heavy thumping footsteps continued up toward me, I shouted out again, "Don't think I'm frightened of you! I know it's you!"

Then I heard my husband's voice through the window. He was outside in the garden! There was no one else in the house but me. I didn't stop to think. I yanked open the bathroom door and hurtled down the empty staircase. There was nothing to be seen, but the air was frigid. I took a lot of persuading to go back inside my home. My husband didn't laugh at me. He was very supportive. It was almost as if he knew how I felt. I didn't know it at the time, but he'd had a scary experience of his own that he wasn't prepared to admit to me until years later.

More than twenty years after we left Linton on Ouse, he confessed to having had a ghostly incident at the RAF base. He was too ashamed to tell me at the time. He'd been so badly frightened by the experience that he just wanted to forget it and pretend it never happened.

He was doing a week of guard duty, patrolling specific areas at regular intervals throughout the night, alone and on foot. In those days the guards were armed only with a pickaxe handle, but that was no protection against what he encountered that night. His patrol route took him along a very dark path. He was on his way to check one of the sites when he heard something strange in the distance. He stopped to listen. The sound was coming from the trees at the other side of the runway, and sent chills down his spine. Women were screaming. Lots of women were crying out in agony, relentlessly wailing in abject horror and despair. It shook him to his core. His immediate thoughts were that something terrible had happened, and he had to help them.

He hesitated for a second, torn between going to the woods or going for help. He would have to run the mile or so to the woods at the other side of the runway in the dark or go back to the guardhouse for help. He decided to go for help, as common sense told him that such a commotion would need more than him alone to deal with whatever had caused it.

He admits that he must have looked a sight when he appeared at the guardhouse. He was out of breath, white as a sheet, and shaking like a leaf. He blurted out what he'd heard, reporting as much as he could remember about the direction the sound had come from, and how far away he estimated the incident could be. He was convinced that an accident had occurred in the woods. Perhaps a plane had gone down, or a bus had careered off the road. He was full of logical explanations of the horror that might be awaiting the team of guards selected to go and investigate. He was amazed at the response from his superior.

The sergeant told him to have a cup of tea and a smoke and forget all about it. My husband protested, insisting that someone should go and help those women. The sergeant explained that many guards had heard that sound before. "Those women are way past any help we might be able to give them." He told my man, "There was a WRAAF block over there during the war. It was bombed. They all died in the fire." My husband was not convinced, and argued that he had heard real women. He didn't believe for a minute that he'd heard ghosts.

"Go back there. Go and listen again," the sergeant told him. "But don't expect me to come with you; it's bloody cold out there."

My husband went back to the spot where he'd heard the screaming. He stood, straining to listen for the sound, but it was silent. There was no wind, not even a breeze to carry the noise away. It just wasn't there. He had to accept that what he'd heard were phantom screams from women who'd burned to death many years ago.

After he'd told me this story, more than twenty years after it had happened, I asked him if he'd ever seen or heard anything else while we were at Linton on Ouse. He sheepishly admitted that he'd seen the ghostly officer in the control tower once. He'd passed him on the stairs, and thought he was just another officer on duty. Then he realized there was something odd about him. He turned to take another look but the officer had vanished.

I asked him what was odd about the officer, but he couldn't remember. "Maybe the uniform was slightly different, maybe I realized he wasn't really there. I don't know what it was that made me look back, but it scared the living daylights out of me to see that he wasn't there at all."

I have many memories of our time at Linton on Ouse, both good and bad, but I'll never forget the memories I have of our ghostly encounters. They still have the power to send a chill down my spine.

I've had a pretty eclectic career, mostly based in the design industry. I now do web site design for small local companies. It keeps me on my toes between bouts of writing.

I discovered a love of writing when my children were small. Writing time was me time. It was a selfish indulgent hobby that kept my identity intact during the mad whirlwind years of being swamped by motherhood. However, the hobby grew at the same rate as my children, and over the years I've enjoyed a modicum of success, seeing my work in magazines, and occasionally winning competitions. I write about anything and everything, both fact and fiction, producing work ranging from children's stories to historical walks, from ghosts and aliens to love and romance. When I'm in the middle of one writing project, I'm already planning the next one. I have yet to succeed in getting one of my many novels published, but being the eternal optimist, I live in hopes that one day my work will fall on the right desk at the right time.

Having this ghostly account published here is yet another step on the writing ladder for me. Since my encounter with these unexplained happenings, I have experienced many more, "other-worldly" occurrences. So many in fact, that I could write a book... now there's a thought. Could that be my next project?

The Ghosts of Bachelor Grove Cemetery

by John Sobieck
Illinois, United States

Bachelor Grove Cemetery is known by many ghost research societies and casual ghost hunters alike as being the most haunted cemetery in the United States. I had heard all of the tales, ranging from the ghost cars seen on Midlothian Turnpike and the two-headed ghost that appears out of the murky pond near the site to the man who comes dashing across the pathway that leads to the graveyard only to disappear moments later. And who could forget the woman who cuts off the heads of men unfortunate enough to be in the place at night.

I had been to the haunted graveyard dozens of times and had never come across any physical or auditory proof of a ghost. I had taken roll after roll of film and videotape without anything appearing on them. My beliefs were beginning to wear thin and I assumed by now that most of the tales were in fact only tales. My mind, however, was changed on a winter day in 2001.

It was an average weekend for my nephew Mike and me. The weather was cold and rainy, and we figured it was the best time to hit haunted places. No one else would be around. We got together our film, videotape gear, and other necessities. This time I decided to try something different. I brought along a Ouija board and planned on testing it out. We arrived at the cemetery around noon and began our investigation.

The place had remained relatively unchanged from the last time I had seen it. Beer bottles had been strewn along the path to the place, amidst other rubbish, and it had the obvious look of neglect. We made our rounds about the cemetery, flashing pictures and shooting video tape as we saw fit. I had the general feeling of discomfort I had whenever I entered this place. The badly damaged tombstones, ripped from their proper places, had been placed as seats for inconsiderate "party animals." Some sites had been partially vandalized, such as the fence around the graveyard, which was torn and cut open in places. I felt like we were intruding in this place, disturbing the peace. This feeling never went away. I was used to this however, and we proceeded with our business.

The initial videotaping of the cemetery and surrounding areas lasted two hours or so. By then we were cold and wet. A shadow had hung in the sky all day. It was then that I decided to try the Ouija board. I'd tried before to contact spirits at various tombstones throughout the area and I always came up with gibberish, as if too many things were trying to communicate at once.

After an hour of this, we decided to call it quits and head home for a while. We started the long journey home and got a bite to eat. Our plans were to return to the site at around two in the morning.

We got back to the place at about 2:30 a.m. Walking down the path with only our flashlights to cut through the darkness, I could feel a great tension in the place. It was no different than usual, but I still felt on somewhat a greater edge. Fog had settled on the cemetery in sheets. As soon as we entered the graveyard, our troubles began.

As we got through the gate, a lone deer that had been grazing inside bolted upon seeing us. This gave us a big scare, something we laughed off after a moment. What luck! Not a ghost, but a deer had scared us half to death. Something was different that night. The fog was swirling wildly in the air, as if a gigantic fan was blowing it around. I have never seen anything like it before.

About two minutes into the search, I heard a loud groan from where I had performed the Ouija board experiment on a gravestone. It sent shivers up my spine and I flashed my light in that direction, but I could not see through the fog. The groan came again. It was like nothing I had ever heard. I tried to remain calm. The place seemed to contort; the paths from tombstone to tombstone lengthened and shortened in a strange way. I told my nephew that I thought we should leave, but he convinced me to stay. So we did.

We made our way farther in and began hearing the beating of drums. It was a loud constant beating that seemed to come from nowhere and everywhere at once. Again, this was something I had never experienced here. I heard voices in a whisper; they were definitely not those of pranksters but something else. They carried in the wind and I felt even greater fear.

We had made one round around the place and then we heard something moving in the bushes in the distance. I told my nephew that I was finished and I felt unsafe here. He agreed and we made our way back to the entrance. As we headed back, the place began to glow brightly. How, I do not know. We tested to see if it was actually bright by turning off our flashlights. We could see without them. That was the final straw.

We got out of the gate as quickly as we could and began walking down the path. We heard more noises and kept steaming fast ahead. About halfway back we stopped and turned around. The cemetery was glowing brilliantly; from this same point before we could see nothing.

It was then that we saw a white figure coming from the cemetery toward us. It seemed to hover through the woods. The thing looked like a cloud, but it was separate from the fog in the graveyard. It looked like a cloud but was in the shape of a man or woman. It came toward us and we decided not to wait to find out what it wanted. We practically ran out of the place and as we came to the street, we took one last glance. The thing still hovered in the distance. We took off as fast as we could. We considered ourselves professionals of this site, having been there numerous times, and yet we lasted less than ten minutes that night.

That night convinced me that something exists out there I cannot explain. I do not know who or what it was that I saw, but I do know that it was not a living human. I have been to many ghost sites throughout the United States and even the world, but I have never seen anything comparable to this experience.

Bachelor's Grove Cemetery sold me on the fact that ghosts *are* real!

John Sobieck is the author of *Wisconsin Dells, The Horror of the Heartland* (no longer available) and *The Solitary Soldier* (Publish America Books). His writings have appeared in numerous literary magazines across the globe. He is a long-time researcher of paranormal phenomenon and hails out of Chicago, Illinois.

The Halfway House Haunting

by Mary M. Alward
Ontario, Canada

When I was a child, Dad often took us for a drive on Sunday afternoons. A regular stop on these outings was Gammick's Gas Station. It was located on #2 Highway, south of Hamilton in southern Ontario. While Mr. Gammick filled Dad's '56 Ford with gas, Mom would go into the store and buy an ice cream cone for each of us. This often was the only treat we had. We lived in a rural area and only went to town once a month. These outings were special to us. My brother and I loved to visit Gammick's. The store was on the main level, and Mr. and Mrs. Gammick lived above the store. Even if the store were closed, Mr. Gammick would hobble down the stairs when a car pulled in. I will always remember him making his way down those stairs, his striped overalls over a plaid flannel shirt.

When Mr. Gammick died suddenly, his wife closed the store and gasoline station and moved to town to live with her son. My siblings and I were saddened. We missed Mr. Gammick's twinkling blue eyes and cheerful smile. We also missed the peppermint sticks that Mrs. Gammick used to slip to us when our parents weren't looking.

I grew up, married my childhood sweetheart, and moved to town. We both missed the farm but because we didn't have a car, we had to remain in the city to be close to our jobs.

After three years, we saved enough money to buy a '59 Buick. Not long afterward, we replied to an ad in the local newspaper for an apartment on #2 Highway. By this time we were expecting our first child. We didn't want our children to be city raised.

To our surprise, the apartment was the upper story of the old Gammick place. It had been completely renovated and we were delighted to find a familiar place not far from our parents. We moved into our old childhood haunt. Little did we know then how much of a haunt it really was.

Shortly after we moved in, our daughter was born. We had just brought her home from the hospital when we awoke one night to footsteps on the stairs. The old staircase on the outside of the house where Mr. Gammick used to hobble down to greet us had been removed. The new stairs descended from the upper hall to a shared foyer.

Thinking that someone had mistakenly entered our apartment, we got up to investigate. Those were the days when doors were never locked. We found no one in the apartment, so we settled down to sleep once more. As we drifted off we again heard footsteps on the stairs. Upon investigating, we found no one. We were baffled and assumed that we had heard someone in the lower apartment.

The unusual footsteps continued to wake us each night, just after midnight. Though we were disturbed by this course of events, we tried to tell ourselves we were imagining things. Then one day I mentioned the incidents to our downstairs neighbor, Cassie. She looked at me, a frown furrowing her brow.

"Oh, that's just the resident ghost. That's why no one stays in the upper apartment. They have a lot of trouble renting it. We hear footsteps but the ghost never bothers us. Only the people who live upstairs."

I was shocked! I had heard many ghost stories in my day but had never believed any of them.

Cassie looked at me oddly. "You didn't know?"

I shook my head, somewhat confused. If no one would rent or stay in the upper apartment, there must be some truth in the story. But ghosts? I wondered if Cassie was baiting me. I looked at her. She was dead serious.

After that, the strange happenings seemed to increase. At night, after the lights were off, a shimmering orb would float down the hall and into the room where our infant daughter, Michelle, slept. As soon as it entered, she would begin to scream. When I went to her room, there was nothing there. I kept telling myself it must be headlights from the highway.

One day when Michelle was ten months old, I left her in her playpen in the center of the living room while I went outside to hang clothes on the line. I had done this a hundred times before.

Cassie always kept her ears open and if Michelle cried, she would call me. Before I even had half of the clothes hung, Cassie called out, "Michelle is screaming. Sounds like she's hurt."

I raced upstairs, heart pounding. When I entered the living room, I was terrified at the sight before me. Michelle was in her playpen, an extension cord wrapped around her neck. Beside her lay two extra diaper pins that I kept on a shelf near the changing table in her room. How had they made their way to the living room? In fact, how had the extension cord, which ran along the wall under the carpet, gotten wrapped around Michelle's neck? The living room was twelve by fifteen feet.

The playpen was in the middle of the room and she was too young to escape its confines. Fear slithered along my spine. The hair on the back of my neck seemed to stand on end. Something was terribly wrong.

That night the orb of light came down the hall as usual. But instead of entering Michelle's room, it seemed to pass through the door that led to the attic. Eerie noises seemed to fill the apartment. My husband and I decided it was time to investigate the weird happenings that we were witnessing. We were scared to death.

The next day, I left Michelle with my mom and took the bus to town. I went to the Registrar's Office and then to the library. What I found amazed me.

In the late 1800s and early twentieth century, the old Gammick place had been a halfway house on what was then known as the King's Highway. In the early 1920s, a woman had left her husband and run away with another man. They had stopped for the night at the halfway house. The woman's husband had caught up to them there. He had gone up the outside stairway and entered their room. He and the woman's boyfriend had come to blows. The boyfriend had drawn a knife and stabbed the husband through the heart. Then, he had run, leaving the woman to explain her husband's death to the authorities.

As I viewed reel after reel of newspaper articles on microfilm, I realized that over the years there'd been many stories published about the "Halfway House Haunting." It seems that the mysterious happenings in the house had been going on for close to fifty years. The only time the ghost seemed to cease his violent behavior was when the Gammicks owned the property. Why?

I never did find out the answer to that question. We moved as soon as possible, fearing that some harm would come to Michelle.

Was the entity in the "Halfway House Haunting" a ghost or a poltergeist, or was there another explanation for the strange happenings? I guess we'll never know. But there is one thing I do know. To this day, no one stays in the upper apartment of that house for more than a few months. It seems the "Halfway House Haunting" is still going on thirty-three years after we moved from that perfect little apartment on #2 Highway.

Mary M. Alward has been published in both print and online venues. She has been published in *Chocolate for Women* and in several series published by *Guideposts*. When Mary isn't writing, she enjoys spending time with her grandsons, reading, or doing needlework.

Flight to Portland

by Ken Ingle
Texas, United States

It was late August 1983. My partner and I were on an American Airlines flight from Dallas, Texas to Portland, Oregon. I was president of a small Grand Prairie, Texas, manufacturing company, and we were traveling to the Rose Festival City to purchase the company.

We boarded the plane, a DC-8, at DFW Airport. The small plane had no first class section. Our seats started on row five on the left side of the plane. A restroom, crew storage area, and passenger luggage, where I left my carry-on, occupied the space between the exit door and us. I had the window seat, my partner the aisle. Only a small galley fronted the right side seats, allowing four more rows. Immediately behind us sat an Oriental woman cradling a very small baby with, it turned out, a bad case of diarrhea.

The boarding passengers put away their luggage and found their assigned seats but the plane remained at the terminal. Shortly, a flight attendant informed us they were waiting for one more passenger.

After a ten-minute delay, a fortyish lady entered the plane. She, too, carried a small baby, only this one was crying. She took the seat opposite and one row ahead of us. It wasn't until later that we learned she was taking the child to Portland for life-saving surgery. She told us the six-month-old baby had cried, awake and asleep, since its birth and that the surgery was to fix a birth defect.

A surgeon in Portland was one of a few doctors capable of performing the delicate procedure. The success rate was hardly better than fifty-fifty. But without the operation, the child had less than a month to live.

It was not long after takeoff and the attendants had doled out a small snack, when a tall, kindly young man sitting in the seat immediately in front of the crying child stood up. Draped in a drab, ill-fitting, and wrinkled brown suit that matched his hair, he turned to the mother. I will admit he had the most peaceful, angelic look on his face. He held out his large hands and asked the mother if he could hold the baby.

Hesitantly, she opened the pink blanket, looked at the infant, then at the man, and handed him the child. Tenderly, he placed the baby to his chest and rested its head on his shoulder. Slowly, carefully, he wrapped a blanket around it. For over thirty minutes, he walked the aisle from the mother's seat to the galley, those large hands constantly caressing the child's back and head as he spoke to it.

It was interesting to watch the flight attendants and how they were reacting to this passenger. Not once did they interfere or offer to help. I think they were as much in admiration of the events as I was.

Behind me, the Oriental lady was intermittently breast-feeding her child and changing its diaper. The rotation seemed constant: breast feed, change diaper. The smell was horrific. Opening the overhead air vents did little to remove the stench.

Some time went by when I realized the baby was no longer crying. I turned as the mother gasped, hand to mouth. The gentle giant held the child at arm's length, smiled, and handed it to the startled mother, then said, "Your baby is going to be fine." The look on her face when she pulled back the blanket and saw her baby, silent and sleeping soundly said everything her heart must have felt. She cried. The big man touched her shoulder and then stepped the short distance down the aisle to the Oriental lady, placed his hand on her child, and said, "Your baby is well." He returned to his seat.

Here I must admit a little shame. It is beyond doubt that the scrunched-up look on my face clearly showed my disgust at having to put up with the foul smell from behind me. The man in the brown suit gave me a look that all but said "shame on you" before returning to his seat.

As all this was happening, the pilot had informed us that fog had closed the Portland airport and the flight was diverted to Seattle, Washington. He estimated our arrival time at 2 A.M.

I wanted to talk with the man about what we'd all seen but decided to wait until we landed and were inside the terminal. I settled in for the remainder of the flight. I tried to sleep but my attention kept drifting to the tall man in the drab brown suit. Shortly, the plane landed at Seattle.

As we approached the gate, he was the first up and to the front exit. Since I wanted to talk to him, my partner and I moved quickly to the front of the cabin. A small, not five foot tall man was between the giant and me. Before I could make it known that I wanted to speak to the Good Samaritan, a flight attendant opened the door to the cockpit so the pilot could thank him.

The man apparently had no luggage in the carry-on compartment but the smallish man between us did. And he was having trouble getting it out as the cabin door opened. The big man left the plane and headed up the jetway. The small man, realizing I was agitated, stepped into the large luggage area and allowed me to get my two-suiter and leave the plane.

The jetway had a turn in it about halfway along its length and the big man had already disappeared from sight. Hurriedly, I raced up the ramp toward the deplaning lobby area. It was a large room capable of holding a thousand people, but at two in the morning, the gate attendant and an elderly couple had it to themselves.

Exasperated, I asked, "Where did the big man in the brown suit go?"

The attendant and old couple almost simultaneously answered, "Sir, you're the first passenger off the plane."

In June of 1996, I quit the professional world, having owned a company and served as president of another and executive VP of yet another. I have three children and six grandchildren. A former Navy man, I attended college and did some graduate work.

I've completed three novels and am working on two more. Three of these works are adventure/suspense and two, science fiction. In my life, I've experienced love, hate, violence, peace, failure, and success. Being in business did give me a wealth of plots, ideas, and experiences from which to draw.

Business-Un-Usual

Tammy A. Branom
Washington, United States

It is my experience that working with spirits can be quite a challenge. And I don't mean just the liquid kind. When working in an establishment that is haunted, not only do you have the stress of bosses, job duties, and demanding patrons, but, as I found out, you have the jokes, taunts, and malevolence of the ghostly guests of the building to deal with as well.

I worked in a nightclub with as many regular supernatural customers as actual ones.

Everything was fine until new management took over and decided to open a part that had been boarded up and used as a storage area. People warned him not to do it, but he proceeded anyway.

According to those who had worked in the club for a long time, that part of the club was haunted by a group of people who had been shot and killed there in a police raid many years ago. As the story goes, the local and federal authorities were closely watching this particular bunch of mafia-type people. When they showed up at the club to drink and have a good time, they had no idea that they were about to be accosted. The authorities surrounded the place, and as they rushed in, a firefight ensued, pushing back the majority of the group into the rear, dark corners of the club. Although they put up a valiant fight, most of the gang's members were killed.

Subsequently, the club was closed for some time. When all the investigations were concluded, the club opened again. But, soon after, disembodied moans and shadows manifested, taunting the employees. Fearful of the restless spirits, the owner had the building blessed. Unfortunately, this only aggravated the temperamental souls, causing them to lash out at everyone who worked there.

As a last resort, the back part of the building where the deaths had occurred was sealed off. Candles and blessings were always put out to keep the spirits in their designated area and away from the paying customers. The mysticism worked well and the business operated without incident.

This tale did not seem to faze the new employer at all. With a scoff, he dismissed the claims and had the walls torn down and the area renovated, expanding the club by nearly a third. Stored in the sealed rooms were old benches, seats, tables, pictures, and other objects from yesteryear, which were incorporated into the new developments, adding an antique atmosphere.

Well, it seems that along with the bygone furniture and space came the bygone patrons.

Shadowy figures of men paced the floors. Footfalls would scurry by, a breeze trailing in the wake. One spirit, a middle-aged man, would appear at a table. Although pale, he would be a solid manifestation, looking like any other customer. He would order a drink and, on occasion, he would wander around and ask questions about the club and the staff. I was told that he was a government agent that had been killed in the crossfire of the club's notorious shootout.

If a spirit didn't like you, it made it apparent. Items would be hurled at you from any direction. On many occasions, the clock on the wall would fly straight off of the wall at the intended victim, most times hitting its target. At first I didn't believe it. I speculated that the clock was simply vibrating off of the wall from the loud music. But when I saw it shoot straight out from the wall and sail across the room, hitting my husband in the back, I no longer doubted that a ghostly force was behind the assault.

Some of the otherworldly customers liked to tease. I would be tapped on the shoulder, or my hair would be pulled, sometimes hard, and I would swing around to find that there was no one nearby. We had to be careful on the steps to the main floor. There were a few times when unseen hands would shove people just as they were stepping down. If they had been drunk, it would be understandable, but most of the time it was someone who had just come in. After the push, the person would usually look around, agitated, and ask who shoved them. I could never tell them that a ghost had done it.

Most of the time, nothing was particularly frightening, until one evening when another girl (who also worked at the club) and I were in the restroom brushing our hair and fixing our makeup. As she went to exit, a loud, beastly growl rumbled in the room. Terrified of dogs, she ran out screaming, "Dog! Dog!"

I knew there was no dog in the building, but I heard the growl as well, so I searched everywhere, even outside, just to be certain. But I knew there was no dog. I automatically assumed that one of the staff was playing a trick on us, so I proceeded to let them know that I didn't think it was funny to frighten someone who openly admits to being so afraid of dogs.

They all looked at me like I was nuts. Solemnly, each one insisted that they had been nowhere near us, much less growled. The whole incident seemed to make everyone a little uneasy about being in the building alone from then on.

The most humorous aspect of the ghosts in the club was the fact that they apparently used the restroom (at least the women's restroom). Stall doors opened and closed, and commodes would flush, but no one else would be in the restroom.

Blurry outlines of heads and torsos would briefly appear in the mirrors and vanish as quickly as they came. Shadows would pass along the walls of the well-lit room, only to disappear into nothing. Hushed voices would talk and snicker, although no one else was present.

As the apparitions revealed themselves more, tensions mounted within the staff. A couple of us had a bizarre feeling of impending doom while we were in the club. Our perceptions were proved as the club burned to the ground one afternoon. The new management's family was in the building at the time. A son died in the blaze. No true cause for the fire was determined, and ownership reverted back to the original proprietor. I, like the other employees, went to work elsewhere, but when the club was rebuilt, many of us did not return. After all that had happened, we feared to have any part of that club.

I have since moved away from that state, but I have talked with some of my friends who work in the club. They say it's business-as-usual, with nothing unusual.

Since 2001 I have worked as a receptionist for an e-business solutions company. After graduating from Western Business College at age forty with a 4.0 in the Administrative Assistant course, I decided to actively pursue my lifelong dream of writing and took the *Writer's Digest* Novel Writing workshop. Many rejection slips later, I sought to expand my writing capabilities and am now enrolled in the Long Ridge

Writer's Group "Breaking Into Print" course for short stories and articles. My husband, Scott, is my greatest support. We live in the Columbia River Gorge in Washington, where life is a little slower and a little quieter.

Ghostly Encounter

by Patricia Tallack
Hampshire, England

This is an account of two experiences of a ghostly nature that happened to me while on holiday in France.

In the first, we had arrived at our holiday home in the Var area of Provence, a few miles inland from the south coast. It was a beautiful new house, surrounded by vineyards with a few houses along the dirt lane.

The silence was unusual, no birdsong, yet there were birds in the trees. They would suddenly take off in a flock, but still there was no sound. Then we discovered that all birds were shot to protect the vines. So the birds had learned a strategy.

We enjoy French village life and this time we were near to Ponteves, walking the three kilometers to collect croissants and bread, or visiting the nearest town of Barjols for our other needs.

One evening we settled down late to sleep. As I closed my eyes, I heard a distinct sound of what I can only describe as an encampment with the noise of horse harnesses chinking and an air of business such as you would expect with people relaxing or busy with their preparation for the night. I heard voices and distant singing.

Thinking that a neighbour must be having a party or a radio was playing loudly, I opened the window to check outside. This was no easy task for we had windows with heavy wooden shutters to open. I leaned out, listening for the party. The night was black and there was complete and utter silence.

Having closed everything, and annoying my doubting husband immensely with my activities, I lay down again, convinced that I had imagined it. I had not been drinking!

Once more the rattle of harnesses came with the feeling of being in the open air and experiencing the atmosphere of a camp and movement of animals and people. But there was no vision with this.

Eventually I heaved a sigh of puzzlement and fell asleep, for there was nothing unnerving about the sounds; in fact, they were strangely soothing.

The next evening it was the same. I investigated outside, this time dragging my husband into the open air to listen with me. He could not hear anything — and neither could I. We returned to bed and, once again, I fell asleep to the sound of the camp.

When I returned home to England I showed a photograph of our site to a close friend who is psychic. He told me he could pick up the tinge of the two popes. That was in the thirteenth century and the time of much activity between Rome and Avignon in particular. Where we were situated, in a valley halfway between the border of Italy and Avignon, would have been a likely place for the Roman soldiers to camp. I can honestly say I was transported back to that time for just a couple of evenings. We returned home after the second night's experience; otherwise I wonder whether more would have occurred!

The second ghostly encounter was during another visit to France, this time in Brittany. A friend had allowed us to use her cottage for a short holiday. It was in the depths of the country but near to a farm. Though the people at the farm looked after the cottage when she was not there, she was still very cautious. When we arrived it took us quite a while to get the place opened up!

It was a very old cottage and had once belonged to a well-known French opera singer who had used it as a retreat. She had died there, some say of a broken heart, after her husband had left her for her secretary.

The ground floor rooms were bright and airy — a spacious living room, tiny kitchen, and a small bedroom. The spiral staircase in the corner of the room — a popular means of reaching and utilizing a roof space — led to a huge bedroom with the deep apex of the roof visible.

We settled into the comfortable cottage, and met the young farmer's son who came to cut the grass and practice his English on us. He was due to go to college in England the following year.

As in the Var, it was at night that the ghostly noises started, but this time my husband heard them too! The first two nights had been uneventful, though rain beat hard on the roof above our heads and we wondered how watertight it was. There were a couple of leaks but strategically placed bowls took care of that.

On the third night the weather was quiet and calm. I had put out the light and lay gazing up into the black of the roof, hoping there were no mice or rats to skitter about the rafters, when a steady knock, knock, knock, came from the side, I would guess about the level of the eaves.

I turned the light back on, breathless and nervous. My husband dismissed it as a drainpipe rattling outside. But it wasn't, I was sure. It was like a steady tap of high-heeled shoes. A measured tread of someone pacing in a slow and regular rhythm. But when I put the light on, it stopped. It began as I turned off the lamp, and stopped when it was on.

We slept with the light on that night.

Next night it was the same. I began to suspect a local teenager or someone was playing tricks. I crept to the outside door, opened it quietly, and stepped outside. I don't know what I expected to find! Someone with a long pole tapping at the roof? I walked all around the site but there was not a soul.

I persuaded my husband to move down to the little bedroom next to the living room — where I buried my head under the pillow and eventually fell asleep.

We reported this mysterious noise to the farmer's son, who shrugged his shoulders and suggested it was the hot water pipes. But there were no pipes where the noise came from.

We left early, after restoring the cottage to its former carefully locked and bolted safety. But I think the ghost of the opera singer was still able to walk there.

When we reported this to our friend she was perturbed — never having had anything like that happen to her! So why were we chosen to hear the "footsteps"?

We have holidayed in France many times, always in remote cottages, and have never experienced any other ghostly events; otherwise I would have begun to think France did not want us!

Patricia Tallack lives at the edge of the New Forest in Hampshire, England, but gets her inspiration for writing from visiting her favourite places — Cornwall and France; though she needed no inspiration for her ghostly encounter, for this actually happened on a visit to Provence. Patricia worked for the government until she retired, then she completed her Batchelor of Arts (Hons) with Open University and, at last, found time to do some serious writing. She has had several poems and articles published and written three plays and two novels, which are yet to find a publisher. Married with two sons, her family comes before all else. She finds cooking very therapeutic and she loves to create meals for her family and friends. She is deeply interested in spiritual healing and has been helped by healer friends many times.

The Legacy

by Carol Sharpe
British Columbia, Canada

It was a three-story home with a basement, built at the turn of the century. The tall gabled roof peeked over the large oak trees and the well-manicured shrubs. The house had four levels. My aunt and her family had the top three floors and my family lived in the basement suite. It was cozy with lots of hidden spaces. The fireplaces in each room added to the warmth because central heating had not been added to the house.

My mom wasn't too excited about living there. She felt uneasy each time she visited the house. "I can't explain it. But there is something wrong here."

"Gert, there you go again with those feelings. What could happen here?" Dad smiled.

"I guess I'm being silly," Mom said softly.

So we moved in. My cousin John and I would find the most secret place to hide, read our books, and play snakes and ladders. My favorite book was *Alice in Wonderland* and John's was the *Hardy Boys* series.

The the wonderful smells of cookies or bread always permeated the house. Aunt Ann would call us to come and have some fresh bread with homemade strawberry jam.

I was always told that I had a wonderful imagination because I would write fairy tales and grab anyone who would listen to me. That was to be my downfall. No one took me seriously when it came to telling tales about the strange things I saw in the basement.

At the side of the house there was a space that was added on to keep the coal and the vegetables. It was called the pantry. I hated going there for the coal. I couldn't explain it; it just made me feel uneasy. I would rush in, scoop up the coal, and throw it into the scuttle.

One time I went to get the potatoes for supper. As I turned on the light a mist hung over the back side of the room. It moved from side to side. I thought it was smoke so I ran to the kitchen and told Mom. She hurried to the pantry, but the mist was gone.

"Are you sure there was something there, Cass?" She eyed me suspiciously.

"Yes, Mom. It was at the back of the room."

"That's strange. I'll get Dad to check it out."

Dad checked behind the shelves but nothing turned up. "Might have been something seeping in the room from outside."

One evening my cousin John was staying for supper and Mom asked him to get potatoes from the pantry.

He was gone for five minutes. Suddenly he was screaming at the top of his lungs. We all ran and there he was sitting on top of a large box and yelling, "Leave me alone!" Dad grabbed John and held him.

It took Dad five minutes to calm John down. John kept pointing to the corner of the room. He couldn't speak. He just kept shaking his head and pointing.

Dad carried John to the kitchen where it was nice and warm. He was shaking from fear.

"What happened, John?" Dad rocked him back and forth.

Slowly John responded. "I turned on the light and started toward the potatoes and suddenly a woman was sitting on the shelf behind. She was all dressed in black and kept smiling at me.

Suddenly she reached out for me. That is when I started screaming. I was so scared — she looked so ugly."

Mom and Dad looked at each other in awe. What was going on? Did he really see this or was he imagining it?

Again Dad searched the pantry to find a sensible explanation. He scratched his head. He usually did this when he was confused.

"Gertie, I don't understand what's going on. Cass and John don't lie. What is happening?"

"Let's check with Ann and see if she can help us."

"Yes, there have been strange things happening, but nothing to be scared of. It's an old house, maybe that explains it." The look on my aunt's face didn't convince Mom.

"I hope that's all there is to it for all our sakes."

Two weeks later I was awakened by a persistent noise in my room. I could see a rocking chair with a woman going back and forth. I peeked over the covers and she was watching me. She stood and started walking toward me. I jumped out of the other side of the bed and ran into my parents' room. I startled them, as they were both asleep.

"What's the matter? Are you okay? Are you sick?" Dad yelled.

I was shaking. Dad wrapped a blanket around me and waited for me to talk. I explained through sobs about what I saw. Dad thought it might be that I was still upset because of John's experience.

"Ted, there's something evil going on! I felt it the first time I saw the house. We've got to find out what has happened here."

For the rest of the night I slept at the foot of Mom and Dad's bed. I kept hearing the chair rocking back and forth.

The next day Mom called the parish priest to see if he could shed some light on this.

When she explained about the episodes that were happening the priest frowned.

"Gertie, that house has been around for years. It has had four owners and each one would tell stories. I don't know if that was for entertainment or if they were true. I have an address of a previous owner and maybe she could help you."

The next day Mom was busy washing dishes. I was doing my homework at the table. She screamed. I looked up and saw a hand grasp her by the wrist. With lightning speed Mom grabbed me by the arm and dragged me out of the room and upstairs to Aunt Ann's kitchen.

"My God, Gertie, you look like you have seen a ghost."

Gasping, Mom replied, "You bet I have and just look at my arm." Her whole arm was red and bruised. Mom explained what had happened. Aunt Ann crossed herself.

That afternoon Mom went to the address of the woman the priest had given her. "Please come in, Mrs. Mitchell. How can I help you?" the woman asked.

When Mom gave her our address the lady's face went ashen. She couldn't speak for a moment. "Are you living in the basement suite?"

"Yes, for about a year now. Can you tell me anything about the house?"

"We lived there for two years. It was the most frightening time of my life. The children kept seeing things. At first we thought they were making it up, but we finally realized they were telling the truth. It all started in the add-on at the back of the house. Every time one of us entered the room something strange happened. Frightening apparitions appeared to all of us, especially the children. It seemed to stay in that one area for a while but later moved into one of the bedrooms.

"I found some history on the house. Apparently the first owners had a daughter who was mentally retarded. She would have fits of anger and the parents would put her into the basement for punishment. One night she escaped and killed her parents.

"The house was supposed to be torn down because it was said to be evil. The next people who bought it liked it so much they kept it the way it was. They figured it was just stories made up."

Mom sat with her head in her hands. "That house is evil. Someone will be killed if we don't do something about it."

Mom went home and recounted her story to Aunt Ann. "Oh Lord, Gertie, that is terrible. What are we going to do? It seems to affect the basement, not the other part of the house."

"I know what we're going to do. We will be packed by tomorrow."

"No! Gertie, you all will move upstairs. There are three bedrooms on the top floor that no one is using. I don't want you to leave."

We packed and moved up there as soon as we could. The house settled down. My nights were peaceful for the first time in months. Three months later we bought a nice cozy home. I often wondered about the old house and if it was more serene now.

Aunt Ann hired a carpenter to remove the add-on and seal up the basement. A year later they sold the house. A new family moved in, but they put the house on the market in one year.

It's a small town and people still discuss stories about the old house while sitting on their porches, sipping lemonade. Neighbors say they hear weird noises coming from the property, but then again it could be their imaginations.

In the meantime the house still sits at the top of the hill, patiently waiting for its next owner.

I started writing at the age of eight. I took a break until the age of sixty and continued on to receive my Creative Writing diploma. My first publication was with *Chicken Soup for the Canadian Soul.* I have been published in different anthologies, newspapers, and magazines. My writing is now taking a new road toward nonfiction writing about social issues. My greatest achievement in life is being the proud mother of five children and ten grandchildren.

The Graveyard Shift

by Elizabeth L. Blair
Arizona, United States

I was pulling my black roller bag down the aisle of the 727. I was ready to go hit the beach. We had a two-and-a-half-hour flight to the Bahamas. In four hours, I had figured, I would be lying on the white sands soaking up the rays and eating conch fritters for lunch, thinking being a flight attendant is the best job in the world.

I was about halfway down the airplane when a head popped up from behind one of the seats. I jumped, obviously surprised. "What are you doing?" It was one of our mechanics.

"Just installing a new strip of floor lighting. I'm just about done," he said.

"Am I the first one here?"

"Stephanie was here but ran up to get some coffee. We crossed paths in the jetway."

"You look tired. Have you been here all night?" Most aircraft get their repairs in the wee hours.

"Yeah, it was a long night. The aircraft is in good shape, though." Wearily, he stood up and stretched. "Actually, have you heard the stories of this particular plane?"

I had a feeling that I knew where the conversation was going. "Is this the plane that has a history of strange occurrences? Isn't there some kind of interesting story that comes along with this plane?"

"Actually, I'm not sure what the story is, but this is the plane everyone talks about."

"Have you ever witnessed any thing paranormal yourself?"

"Sure, several times." He looked around the aircraft.

"Like what?" I had heard of the odd encounters but I had never met anyone who had experienced them.

"Well, every time I work in the cabin on the graveyard shift, no pun intended," he said, chuckling, "I hear footsteps running up and down the aisle. When I look, no one is there. I'm not the only one who has had this happen."

"Really?"

"Cross my heart." He made the motion across his heart. "I think pretty much every mechanic who has worked on this plane has a few stories to tell. Missing screwdrivers end up in strange places and wrenches have been found in seatback pockets on rows we weren't even working on. I've even seen the oxygen masks pop out from the compartments for no good reason. Some of the guys pass it off as our imaginations, but I'm not so sure."

"What else has happened to you?" I asked. My curiosity was piqued.

"Well, the most common are the voices."

"Voices?"

"We end up feeling like fools because we all keep yelling out, 'What?' to each other because we keep hearing our names being called and there's never anyone around. Sometimes it sounds like a woman singing. Crazy stuff."

"Do you tell us flight attendants these stories just to freak us?" I asked, not convinced.

"Trust me. One day you'll encounter a freak incident and you'll come running back to me to tell me how right I was. I was the same way when I first started here and was told the tales."

I laughed, "Okay, I believe you. As long as it's not in-flight." I put my suitcase in the overhead bin.

"That's what is so strange. It never happens in-flight. I think it's because the engines are running. So if someone were whispering your name you wouldn't hear it. Those 727s are loud."

A few moments later the rest of my crew showed up and we had our usual crew briefing about meals, special passengers, and weather. A short time later we took off for the beautiful island. We served a choice of cheese omelets or French toast, both with sausage. Our passengers were wonderful and the flight was smooth. When we arrived on the island, we bid good-bye to our vacationing passengers. Deplaning took a while longer than it should have. The island only had one working airstair, which was pushed up to the front entry door. When the last family made its way down the stairs the crew members gathered their belongings, looking forward to a lovely layover. We carried our bags down the airstairs.

When I arrived at the last step I turned to one of the other girls behind me and said, "I forgot my water bottle. Will you keep an eye on my bags? I'll be right back." I ran up the airstairs and hurried down the aisle toward the back of the aircraft. I pushed the blue curtain aside and entered the galley. I opened the compartment where my water with lemon slices was sitting. Just then I heard someone I thought was the captain call my name.

"Yes?" I responded. I heard my name again. "I'm coming. Did you need me to grab you something from the galley?"

He didn't answer. I pushed back the galley curtain and peeked into the aisle. "Captain? Hello? Did someone call me?" The door to the back lavatories was open and both were empty.

I don't know why but my heart began to race. There was no one there. My mind raced back to the morning conversation. I walked to the front of the cabin while checking every row for a cleaner or prankster crewmate. I peaked in the front lavatory and the cockpit. The aircraft was completely empty.

When I joined the crewmember watching my bags at the bottom of the airstairs I asked if anyone had returned to the aircraft while I was in there. "No, the pilots are already on the way to the crew van as are the other two girls."

Just then one of the local airport workers appeared. "Is everyone off the aircraft? Can I bring the cleaners on?" The plane wasn't scheduled to leave for a few hours. Walking up behind the man was a group of workers with cleaning supplies and vacuums.

"Sure, everyone's off."

"Oh, okay. You girls have a good layover."

We continued our walk to International Customs. I turned around and looked at the aircraft.

"What's going on? Did you forget something else?"

"No. I just thought I heard someone calling me when I went back to the plane — that's all," I said.

"That reminds me. This morning I was the first to arrive at the plane. As I was stowing my luggage I heard someone call my name. Actually, it was more like they were singing it. The mechanic had just left to get a light fixture and none of you were here yet. I grabbed my purse and left."

"That's exactly what happened to me," I said, wide-eyed. "Actually, I thought one of you were playing a joke on me. The voice was so clear."

"Yeah, so was this one. Have you heard the stories of one of our aircraft?" Stephanie asked.

"Actually, I have heard the stories and to tell you the truth, this is the plane. But between you and me I don't think they're just stories."

Elizabeth L. Blair is a regular contributor to the *Haunted Encounter* series. Her work has appeared in many on-line and print publications including the *Christian Science Monitor*, *Chicken Soup for the Bride's Soul*, *The Dollar Stretcher*, and many others. Currently, she is perfecting her first book about her humorous journeys in the airline industry. She lives in Tucson, Arizona, where she is happily married to her husband, Jeff. She has two stepsons and is expecting her first baby in June 2004. She can be emailed at elblair99@yahoo.com.

He Visited Me

by Sigfreid V. Paguia
Pasig City, Philippines

The night before January 13, 1992, while I was sleeping, Matthew visited me in a dream. He was outside the school when I got off the school bus. I looked at him and asked him why he was out. I added that we would be late for school if we didn't hurry up. He looked at me, his hands inside his pockets, his right foot kicking pebbles on the ground. He said he was waiting for me, to say good-bye. I was puzzled by what he said and asked him why. He just stared at me and then walked away. The school bell rang and I woke up realizing that the sound was coming from my alarm clock. It was weird but I thought no more of it.

The school bus arrived and picked me up. Everybody was unusually silent. I sat in the front seat, minding my own business. When my classmate Hazel sat beside me I asked her what was going on in school. I'd been absent for a week due to illness.

She looked at me and I realized that she had something important to say but just couldn't say it. I asked her what it was. Before she spoke, she sighed, and then she told me she had something bad to say. I told her to just say whatever it was. She told me that Matthew was found dead in his room late last night. My mind went blank. I couldn't think, speak, or move. I was in shock.

I came out of my catatonic state when I saw Matthew's house. I told the bus driver to pull over. He did, but only after I stopped yelling. I stepped out of the bus despite the protestations of Hazel and my busmates.

I ran to Matthew's house and rang the doorbell as hard as I could. His mother opened the door and saw me. She hugged me, and told the driver to tell the principal that I was with her, before leading me inside the house. In their receiving room, I saw Matthew lying in an open casket. I ran to him, held his hand, and just stared at his face. She asked me if I was all right. I told her I wanted to be alone with him. She left and I stood there holding his left hand.

I don't know how long I stood there in front of his casket when I felt someone touch my left shoulder. I looked around and saw it was Matthew standing beside me. I asked him if he visited me last night. He just nodded. I looked at his body lying in the casket and I asked him why. He didn't reply. And then he was gone.

I kept calling his name until his mom came to the room. She hugged me and told me to calm down. I told her that Matthew was here, but she kept telling me that my classmate was dead. I insisted that he visited me but she said it was grief manifesting. I assured her that it wasn't just my imagination, and she hugged me again as I broke down in tears.

Ten months passed since we laid Matthew in his final resting place. I'd learned to accept what happened to him and move on with my life, and I was busy with college. Everything was great until the day of Matthew's birthday — November 13. Two days prior to his birthday I was rushed to the hospital. I couldn't breathe and the right side of my body was temporarily paralyzed. In the emergency room the doctors told me the immobility that I was experiencing was due to insufficiency of oxygen. An hour after they put a nebulizer in my mouth, I was able to breathe on my own.

The doctors couldn't understand why it happened; I'd outgrown my asthma when I was seven years old. They kept me in the hospital for observation before signing my release forms the following day. Two days passed and I was feeling great. But my mom insisted that I needed plenty of rest and she wouldn't let me out of my bed.

Morning of November 14. After eating my breakfast and taking my medicine, I went back to my room and returned to sleep. I heard someone calling my name and when I looked at the window I saw Matthew. I asked him what he was doing here. He told me to come to the window. I got up from the bed and walked to the window.

When I got to the window, he reached for my hand and held it tightly. He began pulling my hand through the window. I told him to let go, I was hurting. He said he couldn't because he was taking me with him. I told him that I didn't want to go with him. I was frightened. I knew that whoever that creature was, it wasn't Matthew. I started to fight back, trying to free my hand, but he was too strong.

Then I felt someone grab me around my abdomen. It was my friend Glenn. He had his arms around me and was pulling me back away from the window. After a hard struggle I was finally free. I asked Glenn if I was dreaming.

He asked me how I could be dreaming when my eyes were wide open. I was panting and was shaking hard from fear. He told me he had just come to visit, to see how I was doing. When he was about to knock, he heard me screaming. And that's how he found me by the window, with my right arm stretched outside, struggling with someone or something he couldn't see.

Glenn called my mom and told her what happened. That same day, my mom called a priest and asked him to exorcise the entire house. A week later, when I was feeling better, I went to the cemetery and visited Matthew. I said a prayer and asked for his forgiveness for forgetting his birthday.

A month passed and everything was back to normal until the night before my birthday. Matthew visited for the last time in my sleep, telling me not to worry about him. He told me that he was in a better place.

Sigfreid V. Paguia was born in Manila, Philippines, in 1975 and is the youngest of three children of Emmanuel and Priscila. He has finished two certificate courses in Computer Science and is presently finishing his degree in Psychology.

Douglas, the Elevator Ghost of the Baker Hotel

by Kira Connally
Texas, United States

I was a tour guide at the Baker Hotel in Mineral Wells, Texas, for about five months before it closed to the public in April 2003. I've encountered Douglas several times, and each time was as spooky and surreal as the one before it. Douglas was a real boy who worked as an elevator operator. According to the *Fort Worth Star-Telegram*, on January 17, 1948, Douglas Moore, age sixteen, was severely injured when he attempted to enter a service elevator that had already started up and died a few hours later in the hospital.

That's the official version of the story. Legend has turned Douglas into the victim of foul play owing to a gambling ring he exposed, or maybe the victim of child molestation by an employee of the hotel who was later pushed into the elevator to silence him. Some say the elevator sliced him right in half, and some say he was crushed by the elevator and dragged to the kitchens from where he was transported to the hospital. None of these rumors has any factual background; most likely he died in a simple accident. One thing I will say is true is that he hasn't left the Baker Hotel basement, the scene of the accident.

The first time I heard of Douglas was on my first ghost tour of the Baker Hotel. The tour guide took us into the basement first, and the stairs we used led us directly down to the main service elevator. This particular elevator went from the basement to the top floor, where the ballroom and linen storage were housed. Once the elevator was on its way up, there was no stopping it until it reached the top. The year was 1948, after all, and elevators didn't have doors that would automatically open if there were something blocking the path. In fact, the only doors these elevators had that traveled with them were metal cage doors.

Douglas, being an elevator operator, would have known this, which may lend credence to the story that he was pushed. In any case, it's this basement elevator that led to his death. As we descended the stairs, our guide told us the grisly tale of Douglas being sliced in half, so of course everyone stopped to photograph this spot. My camera was an old Nikon SLR, and for some reason it wouldn't function that day, and hasn't since. It hasn't been to the repair shop yet, but that's beside the point. So there were no pictures for me at the elevator that day.

After hearing this story, I went to the library and dug up the newspaper clipping mentioned above. Once I saw that it was true, I didn't think about it much until I began giving tours and had to repeat the story. I told it without all the rumor thrown in, which must have been good enough because people still stopped to photograph the spot.

During the second tour I ever gave, we heard strange noises coming from the elevator as we came down the stairs to the basement. Upon getting there, all was in order, and I didn't think much of it. It's an abandoned hotel, after all, and not well secured. Any kind of small animal could have found its way in. I took the tour through the rest of the basement and, as we were circling back, I heard what sounded like cables creaking. Still, nothing was out of order, but it had an effect on me. I was starting to believe Douglas really was still here.

About a month later, another tour guide and I were on the fifth floor of the hotel. On every guest room floor, the bank of three elevators opens in the center of the hallway. Floors 2 through 4 have an additional elevator at one end. She and I were alone in the hotel, walking the hallways.

We spent some time in a room on this floor where we thought some paranormal activity was happening, and when it subsided, we left the room and walked down the hallway. As we reached the elevator bank, we both heard the elevator coming up the shaft. Both of us knew we could not be hearing this, so we checked the service area behind the elevators. Nothing was there that could have caused the noise. We walked back to the front of the elevators, and we could hear the faint screeching of an elevator coming to a halt above us. Quite a thing to hear in a hotel with no electricity! We listened awhile, and nothing else happened.

In early January 2003, during a tour of the health spa area on the second floor, one of the cage doors to the elevator slid slowly open, then slowly closed. If it had only slid open, it could have been dismissed as a natural occurrence. But when it slid closed, I thought of Douglas. I had a camera handy this time, and the pictures do show an orb of light inside the elevator in several frames, moving right along with the cage door. What I wouldn't give now to have had a video camera that day!

The next encounter I had with Douglas was in February of 2003. I was at the hotel with a group of friends and one man I had never met before. We were doing the usual ghost tour stuff, and when we headed down to the basement, that man wanted to call Douglas's name in front of the elevator. Everyone else in the group loudly voiced what a bad idea that was, and the man decided to wait. We thought the issue was over, and we went on through the basement, taking pictures and trying to capture ghosts on video.

As we were leaving the basement, we stopped in front of the elevator so someone could catch up with the group. While we were waiting, the man yelled, "Douglas! Come out here! Douglas! Show yourself!" There were three people lined up on the stairs, with me closest to the elevator.

As soon as the words left his mouth, the coldest air I've ever felt went whooshing past me, and it brought the woman next to me, Lisa, to her knees, as if she had literally been punched in the stomach. It hit her so hard she slid down the wall. She was a riser up from me on the stairs, and when I grabbed to steady her, I got a handful of her butt! It's a good thing, though, cause she would have fallen down the few risers right into the elevator door, and who knows what would have awaited her there!

The whole feeling of the place changed. It became heavier, darker, somehow. There was a lesson learned that day: Do not let people who enjoy taunting ghosts come on ghost tours with you!

The last time Douglas made himself known was the last week of April 2003. It was a Friday night, and we were holding a rally to draw public attention to the fact that the Baker Hotel was closed and in danger of condemnation. We had about fifty people come through that night, and once it quieted down, another tour guide, Allison, asked me to walk around to the back of the building with her. We went to the circular drive area where delivery trucks at one time could drive directly into the basement to unload. The drive faces the whole back side of the building, and is actually over part of the basement. She and I headed back there with just her video camera. It was quiet when we got there, and she set her camera on a tripod, and we just listened, watching the LCD screen for darting orbs or any other anomalous phenomena. After about five minutes, a grumbling noise came from the ground beneath us. It slowly got louder, and then moved up. It truly sounded as if somehow the elevator was on its way up the building! We listened in awe for what felt like an hour, but was more likely about ten minutes, and then four more people walked back to where we were.

The noise stopped, and there was a darting orb on the camera's LCD screen. Two of the four people who joined us walked off, and just as suddenly as it had stopped, the noise started again. All of us dropped our jaws, and slowly the noise moved from up high where we had last heard it back to sounding as if it came from beneath our feet in the basement. If that was Douglas's last stand, I have to say, it was a good one.

Kira Connally lives in Mineral Wells, Texas, and works as an optician. She grew up in a family that could see and hear spirits, and spends her free time searching for ghostly activity with a group of friends in the Fort Worth area. Her ghostly adventures can be found at www.blueivvy.com, and she can be contacted at kjc@blueivvy.com.

No Extra Charge for the Curse

by Patricia van der Veer
Merseyside, United Kingdom

For many months we had eagerly anticipated the arrival of bulky brown envelopes bearing a Cornwall postmark. Our Penzance estate agent had offered us a varied selection of properties. Finally, we had made a decision and chosen a granite house in a small tin mining village. We had paid for a comprehensive survey, which showed that the house was free of major structural problems. We then confidently made our offer, which had been accepted.

With our resignations from stressful jobs, we convinced ourselves that most worries were in the past. Tranquil afternoons of tea and scones lay ahead. We had no idea that our vision was flawed and that the house held many secrets.

But for now, my husband, Vic, lay sound asleep next to me in the plane. The hum of the aircraft engines droned on, like bees in a country garden, and did not disturb his slumbers.

I was much too excited to sleep. Finally, after thirty years of living abroad, I was coming home. I glanced out at powder puff clouds and dreamt of our future.

After coming down to earth and collecting our luggage at Heathrow, we boarded a train that carried us out into the countryside. Gradually the red brick houses gave way to a patchwork of bright green fields and stone buildings of varied hues, as we sped toward the South West Coast. Our fellow passengers disembarked at stations whose names made my Canadian husband chuckle.

St. Michaels Mount with its legendary castle appeared through a window, signaling that we would soon be reaching the end of the line: Penzance.

The next day we borrowed a key from the estate agent and took a small bus crowded with people, dogs, and hikers to the small town of St. Just. We walked into a greengrocer's shop and asked how to get to Truthwall.

"Ah, you mean Trughell?" asked the friendly woman. "You must be the Americans. It's just down that hill there, a way."

We walked down the narrow curving road, past stone walls covered by prickly gorse that we examined closely, as cars and farm vehicles passed near to us.

We rounded the corner by a large barn and passed a yard filled with busy hens, beyond which lay a row of five granite houses.

The middle one had a *FOR SALE* sign leaning drunkenly against the front garden wall. The garden was full of tall weeds. An old blue chair lay on its side with stunted wooden legs of varying lengths reaching toward the sky.

We walked up the three stone steps and noted the weathered sign beside the door proclaiming, *CHY GROWYNEK.* This was our dream home?

We turned the long slim key in the rusting lock and walked into a tiled hall. It was cool and dark after the warm sun. The two front rooms were in reasonable shape.

We started to work our way toward the rear of the house. A man in a tweed hat appeared behind us.

"You be the buyers. We heard you be coming," said the man. "I'll show thee the rest." It did not seem that the man expected or required an answer, so together we walked on toward the back of the house.

The air seemed to get colder and colder as the rooms became more and more dilapidated. The last room before the back door looked as though it had been a laundry room. One ancient-looking stone trough shared a corner with an interesting display of multi-layered mushrooms. I nudged my husband in the ribs and gestured upward.

The man with the flat hat followed my gaze. "Look at the size of those mushrooms," I commented.

"Oh, ay!" said the man, as though it were the most normal thing in the world to have mushrooms growing indoors on a ceiling.

We returned the key to the estate agent in Penzance and asked when the final contracts for the house would be signed. He cleared his throat and avoided my gaze.

"I am afraid there is a slight problem," he began. "The owners, in London, have advised us that they are no longer willing to sell it to you at the original price, but will sell for 5,000 pounds more." This process, called "gazumping," is allowed under English law.

My husband and I became very alarmed, but felt that we had no choice but to accept the higher price. The container ship would be here in three weeks.

The following day, we ventured once more into St. Just, which was not quite living up to its name in my mind. We enjoyed a tasty ploughman's lunch in one of the village's four pubs. Our presence as "incomers" had obviously been noted and many local residents smiled at us.

Eventually, I struck up a conversation with a young lady named Tamsin. I explained that we were in the process of buying

Chy Growynek in Truthell. I briefly told her about the gazumping, but that we were still going to buy the house.

"Tch, tch. Probably the curse doing it," she commented before moving on to serve another customer.

My husband's eyes opened wide at her words and he looked alarmed; I was curious.

"Welcome to Cornwall, land of ley lines and stone circles," I said. Vic was not amused. Before we left the pub, I stopped by to speak with Tamsin who was clearing a table near the door.

"What about this curse?" I queried.

"Oh, that," she replied without a pause, putting the dishes on a tray.

"Pauline at the campsite over near you can tell you all about it. She knows her in the Big House that put it on."

"I know just where you want to go next," commented Vic. "This is your country, let's hope you know more about these things than I do. Lead on!"

Pauline, an outgoing woman who ran the campsite over the road from Chy Growynek, was quite willing to tell us the story behind the house, and we had time to listen.

Pauline explained that apparently the up-country owners had not treated the tenants very well, sometimes evicting tenants and refusing to return their deposits. One tenant, Laura, had dearly loved the house and had become a well-known local artist. When she left, word began to spread that the house was cursed, along with its owners.

Since then no tenants had stayed for very long. "Of course there are lots of stories, but who knows," concluded Pauline. We thanked Pauline and caught the bus back to the B&B to think this over.

We decided that we had too little time to find another house, especially since we liked this house and its location. We would pay the increased price and take our chances with the curse.

Four weeks later, the old granite house was ours. However, much work lay ahead before the house became a home and ready to receive guests.

One morning we were sitting in the kitchen, eating our breakfast, when we suddenly heard a loud crash upstairs. I dashed up the wide stairway to investigate. Just as I entered the back bedroom, there was a splintering sound. I fell to the floor as part of the ceiling descended on me. I cried out in shock. Vic bounded up the stairs to find me sitting in the midst of a pile of plaster. I was covered in scratches, but all right.

We needed a builder!

Fortunately, the following day while walking to town, we saw a builder finishing up work on a beautifully converted farmhouse and spoke with him. I think that my scratched face and sad story convinced the man to take pity on us. He assured us that he would stop by later that afternoon.

Bob stopped by as promised and commented that the house was generally sound. A few months' work and assorted building materials and the house would be restored.

Vic in the meantime ordered some building supplies and carefully placed some heavy timbers against a wall in a small room. Timber was precious in Cornwall and rather expensive. Few trees grow in Cornwall because of the presence of granite close to the surface, and a medieval king had used Cornish trees to build his shim. Timber was something to be treasured.

But something in the house had a different opinion, for the next morning we found the carefully placed beams resting in a confused pile on the floor. We had heard no sound during the night.

There were no further unexplained happenings until Bob and his workers started to remove stones from the upstairs wall to place plumbing pipes. Although the outside air was warm, the inside air once again became very chilly. I decided to go and talk with Pauline again.

I asked Pauline to tell me more about Laura and the house. She told me that Laura had devoted her time to painting the scenery while seated by the window of the back bedroom. Was it not possible that Laura was upset at what she perceived as destruction to the home she loved, suggested Pauline?

I began to wonder if that was indeed the case. I always had a strong faith in God and the existence of the world beyond, having been raised with a Scottish great-grandmother. Remembering those beliefs, I decided on a plan.

While Vic was occupied applying render to downstairs walls, I went quietly upstairs to the back bedroom. From the window I could see a ruined engine house and the sea beyond. I breathed deeply and slowly and then I quietly spoke to the spirit of Laura. I assured her that we would care for the house and would do all we could to restore it to its former beauty.

To be on the safe side, I added a short prayer for God to bless this house and keep us safe.

"You okay, Pat?" came a concerned voice from the doorway. It was Bob, probably wondering when the next cup of tea was coming. English workers, I had discovered, worked best if supplied with frequent cups of tea.

I reassured him that I was fine and said that I would go and put the kettle on. The next couple of months were busy ones, filled with plumbers and electricians. Vic and I spent our time cleaning up and painting walls in the evenings. At night we tumbled exhausted between the sheets. Nothing disturbed our sleep.

We had started attending Sunday morning service in St. Just, and afterward going to the pub for Sunday lunch. Sometimes the vicar and his wife joined us.

When the house was about ready for visitors and had a working kitchen. I decided to invite the vicar and his wife for dinner.

Later, during our after-dinner drinks, I broached the subject of curses and ghosts. The vicar did not blink an eye and went on to regale us with tales of hauntings he had experienced. It seemed safe to broach the topic of the curse and what I had done.

Holding his glass of Napoleon brandy firmly, the vicar opened the door of the dining room and started up the stairs. My husband and I watched from the foot of the stairs as he moved silently and slowly from room to room. He came back downstairs and repeated the same exercise with the downstairs rooms. The vicar then came back and sat down next to his wife.

"No negative energy," he pronounced. We were finally convinced when a few weeks later, three beautiful scarlet admiral butterflies arrived in the upper bedrooms. They resided there throughout the winter, until spring, and were our first guests. We do not know what had happened to Laura, or why her spirit lingered at Chy Growynek, but she seemed now to be happy with our presence there.

Although I was born in Liverpool, England, and now have returned there, I have spent most of my life living and working abroad. I first lived in Australia for five years before transferring to Southern California. Although I have a practical side, I am also a romantic, with an adventurous and outgoing personality, who does her best thinking either in the bath or baking bread. After working part time in the medical field in California for many years. I moved with my family to Vancouver, Canada. The next eleven years I spent as a busy police-based crisis/victim service counsellor. With four children nearly grown, I swapped my sensible car for a red sports car and married a Dutch-born Mountie (who happened to be a traffic cop). In 1996, we decided that it was time to say good-bye to the stressful life and move back to my homeland. We chose to move to a former tin mining village in Cornwall, close to ancient stone circles and a turquoise ocean. We dreamed of opening our own tranquil bed and breakfast. Although our new home, Chy Growynek (House of Granite), was solid in appearance, it already held its own uninvited guests. This story is about those early days and the things that went bump in the night.

Badly Shaken Up

by Emma Allan
Alberta, Canada

On a windy autumn evening in 1973, when I was sixteen years old, my friend Jack and I strolled toward the downtown core of the city of Lethbridge in Alberta, Canada. It was my favorite time of year and I was reveling in the scents and sounds of musty autumn leaves scraping in dry gusts across the sidewalks of the oldest and most beautiful residential section of the city. Suddenly Jack stiffened, every part of him tense and alert.

"What is it?" I asked.

"This house," he said. "There's something about this house. I'm getting a very bad feeling from it."

I glanced at the house we were passing and saw an elegant, gray, three-story with columns, bay windows, and wide steps sweeping up to an ornate front door. It was a heritage house, unremarkable in a neighborhood filled with them, built mostly by businessmen for their families at the turn of the century. I certainly felt no strange sensations. But Jack became more and more agitated and, as we picked up the pace and hurried past, he began to gesture nervously as though he was trying to brush something away.

A year later, by a very strange coincidence, my parents bought the house and we moved in.

Being a very practical person and somewhat of a skeptic, I hardly gave the incident with Jack a passing thought. Rather, I was thrilled to be living in such a grand old house. Soon after we got settled, Jack came for a visit. He seemed relaxed and jovial, sharing in the excitement of the charming old rooms as I gave him the tour. It was almost as if he'd forgotten his earlier sense of intense foreboding.

We started in the foyer, which opened into a large front hall, and the coat closet, which held a concealed room that my father had recently discovered. We toured the den with its large fireplace, and the dining and sitting rooms separated by two sets of double French doors. I showed him the old servants' entrance off the kitchen and the stairs leading up to their quarters on the third floor. We climbed the wide main staircase to the broad upper landing, and I showed him my bedroom, my parents' bedroom, and another sitting room. We made our way past the utility room and headed for the stairs to the third floor. Jack reached for the banister and lifted his foot to the first step. Then he froze.

"I can't move," he said, his voice rising in panic. "I can't climb the stairs. Something won't let me."

My immediate reaction was one of exasperation. I was sure he was playing games with me, trying to spook me into thinking the house was haunted. But as I watched he leaned all his weight forward, straining against an invisible barrier. His face twisted into a grimace, his eyes squeezed shut, and he broke into a sweat. He was clearly exhausted when he finally let go of the banister in defeat. I stepped forward and felt nothing as I lightly skipped up a few steps. But I didn't go far, for by now I really was spooked.

As far as I know, Jack is the only person who was never able to climb those stairs. But I couldn't spend time dwelling on that. I had concerns of another nature.

Not too long after we occupied the house my bed began to shake. I often woke in the night to a gentle but distinct rocking. Back and forth; back and forth. Of course I looked for logical explanations. Was traffic rumbling past the house, causing it to vibrate? Was the washer or dryer running in the utility room near my bedroom? Had the furnace kicked in, shuddering throughout the house? None of these postulations proved true. Perplexed, I asked my parents if they'd noticed any strange movements of their bed at night. They had no idea what I was talking about.

In time, I grew accustomed to the bed shaking. It was almost a comfort, like a mother rocking a cradle. I'd wake up in motion during the night and simply think, "Oh, that again." And I'd roll over and go back to sleep.

Then one night things changed — drastically. My boyfriend, Ed, came over and we sat on the front steps, enjoying a pleasant summer evening. Ed was a serious intellectual, and we often had long, drawn-out conversations about the affairs of the world from a teenage point of view. Presently, we entered into a lively discussion about politics. Unfortunately, our perspectives differed, and what I thought was an animated, stimulating debate became for him an argument. I was stunned when he suddenly jumped up and strode off down the steps. He stopped at the sidewalk and turned back to me with a wild and helpless look in his eyes.

"Nobody understands me," he declared, and then disappeared down the street.

I went to bed early, sad and confused.

Sometime later I was shaken violently awake. My bed was jarring back and forth so hard that I was practically pitched from it. This was a force unlike any I'd yet experienced. Gone was the gently rocking bed lulling me back to sleep. Almost immediately I felt a strange tug within me.

"Go to the window," it nagged. "Go to the window."

"Go away," I thought. I was groggy and just wanted to go back to sleep.

"Go to the window."

Try as I might, I couldn't get rid of this ridiculous notion. It made no sense.

Finally, I thought, "Okay. If that's what it takes, I'll go look out the window, then I can get back into bed and sleep in peace."

As I glanced onto the dark lawn below, however, something seemed different. I looked harder, and gradually a huddled form emerged from the shadows. I knew instinctively that it was Ed. I hurried down the stairs and out the door in my nightgown and bare feet. He was crouched beneath a large tree.

"He's upset," I thought, and knelt down beside him in the grass. It was wet with dew.

Dew? Precious minutes passed before I realized that I was kneeling in blood. A large pool of it. Ed had slashed his wrists and in a last desperate act, decided he would die on my front lawn.

With quick action, we were able to save his life that night.

I have no answers for why my friend Jack was unable to climb the third-floor stairs, or whether the same entity that prevented him from doing so was the one who caused my bed to shake. This will remain a mystery. But over the years I've come to believe that whoever or whatever it was didn't want my boyfriend, Ed, to die. That spirit was not malicious or evil. I'm convinced that my bed rocked gently for months before this incident so that I would become used to it, and not be frightened when the time came for me to be urgently wakened in a time of crisis. How do I know this? After that night, my bed never shook again.

Emma Allan and "Ed" eventually went their separate ways. Emma married a man whose career took them to many different communities throughout the province before they finally settled in Southern Alberta, Canada — very near the place this story unfolds. Emma's writing credits include three books, several magazine articles, and a short story produced as a film. Since her first stunning episode when she was a teenager, Emma has tried to avoid supernatural experiences. They still, however, occasionally seek her out in the strangest places and at the oddest moments.

Haunted Sanctuary

by Karen Thompson
North Lincolnshire, United Kingdom

The dog had always barked. That was what made it all so disconcerting. I sat up in the bath, listening closely to the noises she was making. The suds falling from the foaming shampoo on my hair broke the stillness intermittently as I held my breath and strained to hear every stirring from the animal lying at the side of the tub.

Normally she barked at every available opportunity but this time she was whining softly to herself. Peering over the side of the tub, I could see her black and white body dithering with fear and the hair rising on her back as if being pulled upward by unseen hands.

The house had been a godsend. At the young age of eighteen, never having had the happiest of family homes, I discovered this cheap rental at a local agent's. It was a bit of a dump, unfurnished, no central heating and very basic, but to me it was sanctuary.

Besides, it had an "olde worlde" charm and the history to go with it. Originally it had been a village public house and over the years been divided into three separate properties. Mine had been the local butchers, which many of the old folk in the village remembered quite clearly. Across the yard stood a semi-derelict stone building with a tatty tin roof. My neighbour told me that this had been the slaughterhouse and the cellar of my place was where the carcasses had been hung. On investigation, the cellar revealed the rumours to have some substance as I viewed the large rusted meat hooks hanging menacingly from the arched ceiling.

One day, on clearing the weeds from the yard, I discovered a carved stone above the window to the cellar. "I Dearden 1737" it proclaimed proudly. The house had survived many owners in the intervening 240 years and I sat wondering of the lives of those who had inhabited the rooms that I now occupied, visualizing a world void of comforts, of tight corsets, long dresses, and candles in the evening.

But the old place was so very cold, even in the summer months a raging coal fire bought little relief from the dank interior, giving the whole house a hostile and unwelcoming atmosphere. It wasn't helped by the fact that the house stood opposite the local church, a beautiful building of significant architectural importance, but in the evenings the floodlights gave the graveyard in front an eerie orange glow.

Friends noticed immediately. "How do you live here on your own?" they would inquire. "Doesn't it bother you? This place is so creepy." I suppose to a certain extent it did, but to me it was more important to have acquired this refuge. Cold or warm, hostile or benevolent, it was cheap, it was safe, and it was home.

That evening I had arranged to meet my boyfriend at 10 P.M., which left a couple of hours to pamper myself before he called. My faithful hound followed me as usual, and took up her position in the bathroom as I ran the water into the deep tub. I admit to finding her presence comforting when in that room. The situation of the tub meant always having my back to the entrance, and even leaving the door wide open I still felt vulnerable. As I lowered myself into the lukewarm water I could feel the atmosphere change. The dog normally sat up staring at me with eyes wide and ears alert, being thankful for her voyeur participation in the proceedings. Not this time. She began to whimper and slowly lowered her body to the floor, sliding into a position that brought her as close to the side paneling of the tub as would possibly allow. I tried to ignore her. Spending time in this room was not my favourite of pastimes and I knew that my own paranoia and anxieties could only be emphasized by the dramatic actions of the dog. Her whining became louder, stubbornly determined not to be ignored.

I poured the soap onto my hair, becoming increasingly aware of the tension in the atmosphere. She whimpered and I froze in mid-action. "Stop it," I reprimanded pleadingly. She continued and then suddenly fell silent. Soapy hands again fell immobile on my hair, as a draft coming in from the open doorway dried the water droplets on my back and increased the chill in the atmosphere. My whole being was aware that something was very wrong.

The noise came suddenly and was all-consuming. It sounded like heavy old furniture being dragged unceremoniously across antiquated bare floorboards. It was grinding and rasping, echoing through the bare rooms and filling every square inch of space. I was rigid with fear; my breathing became frantic with terror. Two choices were flashing in my head — stay and suffer the ensuing torment from which there appeared to be no escape, or fight this terrifying immobility and run.

Abruptly, I leapt from the water and scooped up the limp dog in one arm, snatching at a towel with the other. The noise continued all around, louder, as I slipped and blundered, naked and wet, down the steep curving staircase, desperately clutching my precious cargo, knowing that if I should lose either I would be too afraid to return. I fell unceremoniously out of the door and onto the porch. The noise stopped.

The dog leapt for the safety of the yard and I wrapped the towel carelessly around my dripping frame before running barefoot after her. I sat, breathless and shaking, on a low wall, quickly looking at the windows of the house next door, knowing that they offered the only possible explanation for the situation and all the while being aware that they would give none. The windows were in darkness, no sign of human life, no answer to my questions, no relief from the confusion and fear. It was no surprise; the building was now a shop occupied only on the ground floor and only in the daytime, but how I wished that lights would have shone from the panelled windows and human forms would be visible, moving furniture around the inside.

The soapy suds on my head dripped woefully to the ground around my bare feet, naked on the hard earth. I had no explanation for the experience, and had no energy to even mentally consider one. It was two hours before my boyfriend arrived. The dried and bedraggled vision that stood before him belied belief. It was two hours more before I could be persuaded to re-enter the building.

No one really questioned my experience that evening, no one who had ever visited the house anyway. Everyone I told, although certainly spooked by the story, never appeared surprised.

From that evening on there was an increasing frequency of unexplainable happenings. The door that led from the kitchen to the staircase would be left open every night as it had a tendency to stick if closed properly. Many mornings I would come downstairs to find it closed firmly and had to shove my way to freedom. Eventually the handle and catch had to be removed after one of the ghostly closings trapped me tight and fast, and I had to resort to shouting out of the bedroom window to customers entering the shop next door to come and free me.

Then items started to disappear, not to move, but to vanish entirely. Packets of cigarettes seemed to be my spook's preferred choice and it was because of this that I finally decided my spirit was a friendly soul concerned only with my health and welfare! The dog seemed more affected by the happenings than anyone. On two occasions, and with witnesses present, she fell into a snarling crouch and stared fixedly at a point on a wall. Then, hackles raised, she would slink around in a slow invisible semi-circle, staring and growling but never moving farther forward toward the wall. This would continue for perhaps a full minute, then quick as a flash, the invisible barrier would be gone and she would run forward, sniffing the floor and wall that moments before she had been too scared to put her paw upon.

I began to live happily with the irregular occurrences. Instances such as cupboard doors banging without any physical assistance, clothes disappearing and then being returned the following day to their original location, buckets throwing themselves, lemming like, down the cellar steps and of course my regular stop smoking campaign simply became part of life's mysterious routine.

Many times friends asked me why I didn't investigate the history of the house, find out what was causing it, if anyone had died there. It had always been in the back of my mind, but to be honest, I didn't care. Whatever was going on was doing me no physical harm, I was no longer afraid, and in a way felt comforted by my unseen companion.

After five years the time to move on finally came. I had a partner; we had bought our own place and were excited at the prospect of central heating, constant hot water, and a shower. But still the old place was difficult to leave. It could never have been described as a comfortable home in the material sense but it had given me the greatest of mental comfort, and I would miss it despite its faults.

We had been in our new home for perhaps a couple of months and I was sitting reading a large broadsheet newspaper. The paper suddenly flew from my grasp as if unseen hands had snatched the paper from me. I ran shouting into the kitchen and my partner ran in from the garden. I was breathless, I couldn't believe it. Was it possible that my ghostly buddy had followed me? I excitedly explained what had happened; he made it quite clear that he thought I was lying, exaggerating at the very least.

The situation got more and more heated and had just reached blasting point when the lightbulb above his head exploded into thousands of tiny shards. It stunned us both into silence until he quietly offered the explanation that bulbs sometimes "do that."

"Not when they are switched off," I pointed out. We stood facing each other from each side of the work counter, each waiting for the other to offer some words of comfort. "Maybe the spirit is not in the building but in the soul," he said.

I'm a rustic forty-something English female who only recently entered the world of putting thoughts to paper because of intense pressure from an American friend who enjoys reading my emails! Several articles and stories have been published but my great claim to fame is writing for the U.K. publication *Car Boot Calendar,* recalling the exploits of trading in the antique and collectibles world. Despite being a serious skeptic of the next life-phenomena, I have to admit that I don't have the answers!

The Green Lady

by Bill Kelly
Illinois, United States

We heard about the Upson Road Cemetery through a newspaper article on land allotments in Connecticut. It had been written by the mother of a close friend of ours. The article had been straightforward enough, listing the size (less than one acre), age (its earliest tombstone was dated 1632), and current status (closed — no trespassing). What the article didn't say was how difficult it had been to get the townsfolk to talk about the cemetery, or why no one ever uses Upson Road anymore.

* * * * *

I down-shifted the Suburban as we ventured deeper into the forests of rural Connecticut. Even with the brights on, I could see beams of moonlight cutting through the trees like supernatural streamers. I remembered reading somewhere that Connecticut is the second most densely populated state in the country. Well, whoever had taken that survey hadn't been here. Breaking up the thick trees lining the dirt road were decrepit stone fences surrounding old farmhouses and wooden barns and mills blackened from decay and fire.

The sign became visible only a few seconds before I had to turn. Stenciled in black on the flaking white paint were the words "Upson Road." My fingers fumbled over the turn signal; the sound of the blinker finally broke the long silence that had dominated the trip. The winding, thin dirt road to the cemetery was without artificial illumination as well.

For a moment, I switched off the headlights and drove purely by the light of the moon. It was an eerie sensation, like floating, and I could feel adrenaline rushing through my body.

At last, the graveyard appeared on the left. The three of us sat in the truck, staring, not saying a word. I made a small pact in my mind with God — I really didn't want to see what we'd come here for. But none of us wanted to show fear in front of the others. We made eye contact and unlocked the doors.

The graveyard itself was smaller than I'd imagined. It, too, was surrounded by a stone wall. There were a few tombstones scattered about, and we were able to make out one date as 1650. And in the back, next to a large tree stump, was where she was buried — the Green Lady.

The legend goes something like this: Around the time of the Salem witch trials, in Burlington, Connecticut, there was a young girl accused of witchcraft. She was put to trial and found guilty. The sentence, of course, was death, but not by hanging. She was to be made an example, a deterrent to others likewise tempted by the devil. So on a cold autumn evening, the townsfolk gathered in the Upson Road Cemetery to watch this poor girl, bound but not gagged, buried alive.

Almost immediately after, people began seeing a green mist in the cemetery and the woods around it. And on occasion, a green apparition of a young woman was seen walking the cemetery grounds and along Upson Road. According to the legend, the apparition was so hideous that those who saw it were driven insane.

Kieran, JD, and I made our way toward the stump. The old, tired earth gave with every step. The dirt, now dug up far too many times, was covered with a thick layer of moss and very little grass. Our minds played tricks on us, making every snap of a twig, insect call, or rustle of leaves sound like the onset of a murderous charge by some heinous miscreant.

Next to the stump was just more decomposing earth. JD picked up a discarded beer bottle and it glistened in the moonlight. We were all shaking even though it was a warm night.

We each commented on the size of our bladders, but dared not venture into the woods to remedy the problem. One of the legends we'd heard said if you urinated or spat on the ground, green mist would rise out of it. We weren't eager to test it out.

Kieran moved first. He took the Ouija board from under his arm and placed it on the stump. We all sat around it, though no longer sure why exactly we were doing this. We each placed two fingers on the pointer and it jumped to life. It made large figure-eight sweeps across the board. The fear in each of our faces confirmed it — none of us were "pushing."

Kieran agreed to ask the questions. He began with, "With whom are we speaking?"

The pointer darted to "m," then "a," then "m," then "a." It resumed the figure eight.

"Are you somebody's mother?" he asked. The pointer went straight to "no," spelled out "mama" again, and resumed the figure eight. Kieran asked several more questions, but the only reply was "mama."

Then I remembered the legend. In my mind I could see, on this very spot, a terrified girl being forced prematurely into her grave… her mother trying to break through the unyielding arms of the righteous mob, desperately trying to save her daughter as the dirt rained down….

Chills came over my body, and the hairs on my neck stood on end. "Kier," I said, "ask if she's looking for her mother."

Kieran understood, and nodded. But as he started to ask the question, we heard a loud crunch in the woods, followed by a repetitive wheezing. We jumped to our feet but could see nothing in the woods. The wheezing sounded like it was getting closer.

Without saying a thing, the three of us sprinted to the car, weaving in and out of the gravestones. I bobbled the keys in my hands while trying to find the right one. The wheezing got closer and out of the corner of my eye I could see the bushes moving. I got the door open and we all jumped in. We left in a hurry.

Kieran was the first to speak. "Did you guys get a look at that?"

"No," I said. "What did you see?"

"I'm not sure, Bill, but when you were getting in the car I looked back in the woods and, well, at first I thought it was a bear, but it was walking. And it was… I swear… ten feet tall."

For about a week, our experience in the cemetery was all we could talk about. But in time, as is usually the case, we rationalized everything. The wheezing was probably a frightened or injured animal, and since we were all a little scared, our imaginations were no doubt working overtime. We told a few of our friends, all the while making fun of our own foolishness. We eventually convinced ourselves there was nothing to be scared of.

As Halloween drew nearer, we couldn't resist making plans to go back. This time we were going to bring flashlights and candles and just sit around and tell ghost stories. But we weren't going to bring the Ouija board, just in case. My younger brother Jon had heard us talk about our first visit and asked if he could go along with us. JD and Kieran didn't mind, so I let him join us.

So almost a month after our first trip we were back out in the Connecticut boonies, off to see a ghost we didn't want to see. The town of Burlington was completely black that Halloween night—

we later found out there was a power outage. We drove by stores lit only by the pale green emergency lighting. The town's two stoplights were not working and the old town hall, normally lit by two exterior floodlights, was a dark, abandoned fortress. The nearly full moon was a brilliant white in a cloudless autumn night sky, providing the only necessary illumination.

We headed deeper into the woods and eventually came to Upson Road. Seeing the street sign caused all the emotions from the last visit to come flooding back into my body, inundating my mind with notions of calling the whole thing off.

JD turned to me and said, "Bill, do we have enough gas to get home?" I could see he was just as scared as I was.

"I don't know, but I just had some," said my brother.

We all laughed, and it helped us forget how scared we were. We drove down Upson Road, determined to have a good time, until we saw that we weren't going to be alone in the cemetery. There was a white Pontiac Firebird parked right outside and we could see four people sitting around the tree stump.

"Maybe we should leave," said JD.

"No, I want to go talk to them," said Kieran.

"No way!" said JD. "Only freaks would go sit in a haunted cemetery on Halloween."

Kieran gave JD a look as if to say, "Wasn't that the general plan?"

Before they could finish their argument, my brother got out of the car and shouted up to the four, "Hey, are you guys psychotic or, like, demented in any way?"

They laughed and we went in the cemetery to join them.

"What brings you guys here?" I asked.

One of them said he had heard the legend of the Green Lady from his dad who used to live in Burlington. They had been coming here for a few years and had a few unexplainable experiences, but had never seen the ghost.

"Have you ever brought a Ouija board here?" asked Kieran.

"Yeah," said one of the guys, "but it didn't really work. All it kept saying was 'mama.'"

Kieran, JD, and I jumped back as if slapped. We told them how the same thing had happened to us. A few people shifted uncomfortably.

"Hey, have any of you ever heard of Deadlyville?" asked one them. We all shook our heads. "Well," he said, "in the 1700s there was a small town called Dudleyville near what is now Canton, a town directly east of here. So, anyway, one night the mayor of Dudleyville frantically gathers the townspeople together. He tells them he was traveling through this area with his family when they were separated, and that he needed help to go back and find them.

"The townspeople wrote that he had a possessed look about him as if he had brought back the devil with him. Which he must have done, because he brought most of the small town back this way with him and none of them were ever heard from again. Dudleyville became deserted and eventually so overgrown that it blended in with the woods only a few miles from here.

"When other people finally came to look for the town, they were terrified to find the insides of the buildings covered in satanic writing. They returned telling stories of a race of hideous giants that now inhabited the forest. They found the minutes from the town meeting where the mayor requisitioned people to look for his family, but said the last few pages were covered in blood and strange writing. From then on, the place has been known as Deadlyville."

When he finished, all I could think about was the thing that Kieran had seen when we were leaving the first time. Was it one of the giants supposedly inhabiting these mysterious woods?

We tried telling more ghost stories, but none could compare to Deadlyville. After about an hour, we were cold and tired and decided to call it a night.

I really don't know what came over me, or dare I say, possessed me, but as we were leaving I climbed up on the tree stump and looked around. I was covered in moonlight and everyone was looking at me apprehensively. I put my arms up in the air and shouted, "Mama!"

Everyone froze in place, staring at me in disbelief. I put my arms down and jumped off the stump. What happened next I will never be able to explain. Just as my feet touched the ground, a scream came from the nearby woods. It was a high, piercing female scream that shattered the brisk October air. It echoed through the night for a few seconds before dying out. I looked around — seven people and then myself — we were all here, so it didn't come from us.

I knew from our previous drive through the area that there were no inhabited areas for at least a few miles and there were no other cars around. I didn't need to think about this anymore. For the second time in as many visits, we sprinted for our lives all the way to the car. All of us except my brother, who sauntered out of the cemetery.

"Hey!" he said. "What gives?"

"Jon! Get in the car, now!" I yelled. His lack of rapid movement was disturbing, but it gave me time to get the car unlocked. My brother finally got in the car and asked what happened. We told him about the scream, but he insisted he hadn't heard anything. He thought we were playing a joke on him. I have since come to wonder if perhaps he didn't hear anything because he was the only one who hadn't been part of a "mama" Ouija summoning.

Once we were out of the woods, I pulled into the dirt parking lot of a small local restaurant. The regular lights were still out, but a dim emergency spotlight cast a fuzzy glow on the ground below. The Firebird pulled in behind us and we all got out.

"What on earth was that?" one of them asked.

We shook our heads for a while, trying to calm our nerves. Our new friends tried to light cigarettes but their hands were shaking too badly. I looked over at them to ask if they had seen anything when I noticed that there were only three of them.

"What happened to your other friend?" I asked.

"What other friend?" they said.

"That other guy — the one who told that messed up story about Deadlyville."

The three of them looked at me in horrific disbelief. "He showed up, like, one minute before you guys did, but from the woods. He told us he was with you and was just making sure everything was cool before you showed up. You mean he wasn't with you?"

A chill went up my back.

"Maybe he was the mayor," said Kieran.

"Don't be ridiculous," I told him, "that story is hundreds of years old."

But of course, we'll never know. We never actually saw the Green Lady, but perhaps it is better that way. There was something unsettling about that place. Maybe that's why no one ever uses Upson Road anymore.

William E. "Bill" Kelly III lives in Chicago, Illinois, with his wife, Laura, and their dog Rudy. A copywriter by trade, Bill has also been an account executive, a U.S. Army officer, a professional actor, a museum super-science demonstrator, a copy/fax room peon, and a religious bookseller (briefly). Bill recently penned his first screenplay, *Hulk Hogan and the Half Eaten Savior.* In addition to short stories, he is hard at work on that elusive first novel. He gets many of his story ideas while hiking the great outdoors with fellow writer Kieran McGowan. It was on the Metacomet trail in Connecticut that Bill and Kieran first decided to pay a visit to what is now known as the Green Lady Cemetery. Bill grew up in West Hartford, Connecticut, and has a math degree (of all things) from the University of Notre Dame in Indiana. Bill would like to thank his family for all of their love and support, including his parents, Bill and Susan, and his siblings, Cindy, Jon, and Katie. But Bill's biggest thank-you of all goes to Laura, the love of his life, without whom he'd most likely be a useless video-game-playing movie junkie.

My Auntie's Ashes

by Ellie Robson
Alberta, Canada

My aunt, my father's youngest sister, was also my godmother. She married a design engineer and moved from country to country, project to project, every few years. My family was military and on the move as well, so I only saw her for a day or two every five years. Even after her husband died, she kept going, living and working and visiting in warm countries from the Caribbean to Australia.

Then my aunt, after staying in one place in Canada for several years, decided to move to England, a journey of more than 10,000 miles. As I hugged her good-bye before her plane left, tears came to my eyes. I knew somehow this would be the last time I would see her. Six weeks later she died very suddenly from an unsuspected lesion on her heart.

The news flashed from family to family across the country, and I knew it had to be true. Yet I had a very strong sense that night that my aunt was still around, shocked and horrified and feeling very lost.

I found myself lighting a candle and assuring her that she was just as welcome in my home now as she had been on her last visit. That night, and for many weeks afterward, my aunt appeared in my dreams about twice a week. She would talk about her life, her marriage, her anger at being widowed young and the years of raising three children alone, her hopes and her fears for those children and her grandchildren, the youngest of whom was barely a year old.

My family is very strong on rationality, and would not ever believe I was getting information from "beyond the grave," but I got into the habit of making notes each morning about whatever I could remember of my aunt's dream stories. Just in case.

My aunt had left no instructions about the disposition of her ashes. Her children gathered in England for the main memorial service and decided to send the ashes back to Victoria, British Columbia, the city where she had lived the longest. Her surviving siblings were living there, too. They agreed to scatter her ashes at Butchart Gardens, a beautiful place that she had loved and often visited.

They would do this in springtime, on what would have been her next birthday. My aunt, in my dream, let me know she was delighted by this plan, but again there was no way to know if I was just putting words into her mouth. My aunt's son (her executor) brought the ashes back to Canada on the plane, and mailed them to her oldest brother in Victoria, thus reversing my aunt's last living 10,000-mile-plus journey.

A short time later, while talking on the phone to my aunt's son, I realized I knew things about his family, and his sometimes-troubled relationship with his mother, that there was no way I could know given the lifelong distance between our two families. I tried to hide my knowledge — I sure didn't feel ready to answer questions about where it had come from — but it was difficult. I felt like I was being steered the whole time I was talking to him, gently pushed to ask certain questions or to get him thinking along certain lines

When my cousin was telling me about a very moving quote from a novel that he had found typed and written out several times among his mother's papers, I told him the author's name

— Rosamund Pilcher — even though I have never read any of her books myself and didn't know my aunt had either. That could have been explained away, but then I really slipped. I referred to his littlest sister, who I had not seen or spoken to in more than twenty-five years, by a joking family nickname that she only acquired fifteen years ago. And then I called him by his mother's secret pet name.

This forty-year-old, hard-as-nails businessman broke down crying.

I felt flat-out awful. I didn't know what to say. Fortunately, he calmed down after a bit. He asked how I had known. I could have lied and said my aunt had mentioned it on her last visit. Instead, even though I was afraid he would be more upset or even angry, I told the truth. To my surprise, he was relieved, not upset. He said he had known his mother would try to communicate if she could, and he had been waiting for some sign that he was handling things the way she wanted. He asked me to wait while he found the quote from the novel, and read it to me over the phone. It said, in effect, "I'm not really gone. I'm just in the other room. I can still hear you, and you can hear me, too."

After that, my cousin and I were in partnership. When he had questions about his mother's intentions over settling her estate, he would ask me. I would sleep on it, and let him know what answers I got. Sometimes I didn't get any, and he would go on his own best judgment.

Then came a real crisis. On the eve of what was supposed to be my aunt's scattering-of-ashes, her siblings quarreled. One refused to go to the Gardens, another wanted the ashes put in a formal columbarium. The third arbitrarily decided to take my aunt's ashes back nearly a thousand miles to a small, northern Alberta town where their mother, my grandmother, was buried. She would leave the very next day.

Although I was wide awake that afternoon and over a thousand miles away, I knew instantly that something was wrong. My deceased aunt was terribly upset at the idea of being tied for all eternity to a cold, desolate town she had never liked when she was alive. I phoned my mother and heard about the fight. I couldn't blurt out that my aunt was furious. All I could think of that wouldn't betray my secret was to ask that my mother stop anyone from doing anything until I had consulted with my cousin. My cousin asked that they keep the ashes in Victoria until he could come there, probably in the autumn, and so it was agreed.

That should have been the end of the matter, but it wasn't. A month before my cousin was to go, the siblings were quarrelling again. This time, my aunt's ashes ended up in a parcel, mailed over a thousand miles to my cousin in the prairies. He brought them to me, adding another ten miles to my aunt's post-death travels.

By this time, if I concentrated, I could hear my aunt's voice almost as clearly awake as I could asleep. And she wanted to be back in Victoria. We set out on the thousand-mile journey back to Vancouver Island, this time by car through the Rocky Mountains. When we arrived there, we didn't contact the squabbling siblings at all. Instead, we drove around for two days, directed by my aunt's wishes, visiting the places she had loved most when she lived there. We covered another fifty miles around the city and its beautiful surroundings.

Then at last, on a misty autumn afternoon, we drove my auntie's ashes the fifteen miles out to Butchart Gardens, had a lovely high tea in the dining room, toasted her with sherry, wrote her name in the visitors' book for the final time, and scattered her few mortal remains at the cove beneath the Gardens, thus ending a post-death journey of 13,375 miles. As the sun settled into the ocean beyond, I heard her voice once again, softly fading until it was indistinguishable from the waves on the beach. She was happy, drifting away.

In the years since then, when opportunity arose, I shared with my aunt's other children some of her last thoughts and wishes for them. My aunt has visited them briefly in dreams, comforting them and even telling jokes. Her youngest grandchildren sometimes report over breakfast that Granny sang to them in the night, although those occurrences are fewer as the children get older. Somewhere out there, it seems, my auntie and her ashes are still traveling on.

I am always grateful that I was able to help her make those last earth-bound arrangements the way she wanted them.

Ellie Robson comes from an English family whose castle, though still standing, has housed none but ghosts for more than 200 years. After years of country-hopping, Ellie settled on the Canadian prairies, where she writes historical fiction and nonfiction. When not writing, she often finds herself mediating between the living and their departed relations, and regularly consults with homeowners, real estate agents, and business people wherever ghost activity is a concern.

A Walk in the Rain

by Keith Carter
Lancashire, Great Britian

I used to go walking with two friends, Mark and Roy. All of us were equally keen to explore the fells of the Lake District and reach the summits, happy in each other's company and following an activity we all loved.

After a couple of years we had done the main areas and began to seek out lesser-known valleys and ridges until our knowledge of this loveliest of England's hill country became familiar to us in all its guises. We didn't ask for good weather although luckily it was often fine on our outings and it was unusual for us to meet heavy rain or bitterly cold conditions.

On the day in question, we had been unlucky for once and as we laced up our walking boots and pulled on our weatherproof gear, we knew we were in for a wet day. I had chosen the walk, the others happy to leave the map and compass work to me. Although they were always ready to raise objections whenever they thought I was forcing them to do too much uphill work. I had decided on a little-known valley in the eastern Lakes that reached like a questing finger into the high hills around the head of Hawes Water. We were in high spirits and kept up our habitual light-hearted banter as we squelched our way into the deserted country of the early stages of our walk.

After an hour or so of walking head-down into driving rain, I saw ahead of us a cottage that was marked on the map simply as "ruin" and, making for it, I told my party that we could take shelter there and have some coffee from our flasks out of the wind and rain. An ironic cheer greeted my words and we were soon pushing open the door to what must have been at one time quite a substantial farmhouse. What outbuildings it had once had must have been pulled down for building stone elsewhere.

Inside there was a table and a bench and someone had salvaged an old settee that was soon occupied by my friends, who were even talking of lighting a fire in the blackened grate. I cautioned them not to get too comfortable as we would soon be pressing on, and was taken to task for being far too strict as a leader.

As we talked and joked there came noises from above our heads that sounded like voices and footsteps of people moving from room to room. This was followed by a heavy scraping noise like a heavy bedstead being dragged across the floor. We conjectured that perhaps another group of walkers had sought shelter like us and were ensconced upstairs. We hadn't seen anyone else all morning, so they must have been there for some time, perhaps waiting for the rain to ease off. Their voices sounded young and one of our number suggested that they could be a group of schoolchildren engaged on an expedition with their teachers, or perhaps teenagers on their Duke of Edinburgh Award challenge.

Roy was always the inquisitive one, never content to take anything at face value, so he went to explore the other rooms of the cottage. Much of the plaster off the walls lay about on the wooden boarded floor and we could hear it crunching under his boots as he went from room to room. Returning after his tour of inspection to where we were spread out like an army on the march, he looked puzzled.

"The peculiar thing is," he said, scratching his bald head, "I can't make out where the staircase is."

"Perhaps it goes up from outside," said Mark, the practical one among us. He was a surveyor for a damp-proofing company in professional life and spent most of his time inspecting old buildings in his hunt for dry rot. "These old farms often had a separate outside staircase. They kept the animals downstairs in the winter. It helped to keep the upstairs warm too."

We accepted this explanation, which seemed to fit the situation perfectly. The voices upstairs were not easy to make out but occasionally a child's treble came through clearly saying, "We're hungry, Mother," or something like it. We exchanged glances, wondering why anyone would bring out a party of schoolchildren on a day like this without sufficient food. At least they were in the dry.

I looked out of the window, the panes layered with decades of cobwebs and, imagining the rain had eased up a little, suggested that we should continue our walk. We hadn't come out to spend our time drinking coffee in ruined farmhouses. There was plenty of good-natured dissent but wet gear was pulled on, rucksacks packed, and we were soon ready for the off. As we left, I thought I heard a baby crying. Pausing in the entrance hall to listen, all was silent. Shrugging to myself, I closed the door behind me and pulling up my hood against the rain, hurried to catch up with the others. They were ahead on the narrow trail and I thought how like infantrymen they looked, plodding up the line with their heavy packs.

Thinking over our conversation about the staircase, I turned to look back at the building, now almost obscured by the mist that was swirling around it. The windows, like sightless eyes, kept back the secrets of this desolate farmstead that must have been a home for generations of farming folk trying to scrape out a living from these inhospitable fells. Perhaps newly married couples had come here to set up home, bring up children, and live out their lives. What dramas had unfolded here, I wondered.

Trying to shake off a feeling of unease, I scanned the cheerless scene one last time.

It was then that I noticed with a sudden and profound shock something I had missed until then. The building had no upstairs.

Who am I? I am a freelance writer based in Lancashire, England. Now retired from a career as a captain of industry, my only subordinates now are my vegetables and my limited control is over my own little acre. My family means everything to me, the delight of communicating with small grandchildren having nothing to compare with it in this life — to see their rapid comprehension, their imagination alive with interest, and their boundless energy is more stimulating and involving than any work ever was.

I love films and plays in equal measure and have kept a list of every book I've ever read. Some years when I was busy earning a living, the list is short. Now that I have more time, I want it to be as long as it can possibly be; there is so much to read. A member of the Outdoor Writers' Guild, I have researched and written two guidebooks, one on *Offa's Dyke Long Distance Path* and the other on the *Pennine Way*, both long-distance trails in the British Isles. I have also contributed to various publications including articles on historical walks in the North of England. I write poetry and short stories and am working on my third full-length novel, titled *The Third Age*, about how a family copes with a father's deterioration and death.

An Encounter on the Railroad Tracks

by Diane R. Schmidt
Ohio, United States

I have never been the type to believe in ghosts. While I had watched *Unsolved Mysteries* growing up and laughed about ghost stories around campfires, I didn't really believe there was such a thing as ghosts. The summer of 1995 changed my mind forever.

I lived in a small town in upstate New York, which was settled in the 1700s. Once a bustling town located near the Hudson River, it is now run down. Shells of businesses line the streets and an abandoned set of railroad tracks circles the perimeter of the town.

I had always been interested in history, and this area of New York was chock full of history and legends. I had heard stories of people jumping off the bridge, in anguish over lost loves, and homes built and lived in long ago that had lost souls roaming their halls. I never got up the courage to venture into one of these old homes. Some of my friends had, and they had never gone back. Even the guys I knew who were considered macho and not scared of anything would not talk about what they saw and experienced.

One warm summer night, I met with my friend Mark to take a walk. I had romantic feelings for him but we were mostly friends. We decided to walk down the tracks and hang out on the bridge, which overlooked the highway. After a few minutes of walking along the tracks, which were overgrown with weeds, we got to the bridge. We talked and playfully teased each other, as we watched the sun set.

On one side of the bridge was a thick clump of trees and the other was the direction we had walked from. We hadn't walked as far as the woods; we didn't know what was down there. This area was very isolated, though. We didn't notice anyone around and thought we were alone.

Around 10 P.M., we noticed a faint light coming from the trees. We stared at it and assumed it was a flashlight and other people were coming up to the bridge. We looked harder as it grew bigger and started to take on a shape, from the bottom up. A pair of feet began to take form, then the bottom of a dress. From what I had thought about ghosts, they just appear in full form. This one was different. The wispy figure took a few seconds to fully appear.

Our eyes were glued to the light as it became not one, but two ghostly figures. The man was dressed in old-fashioned formal attire; it looked like a suit or tuxedo. The woman was dressed in a long flowing gown. They waltzed toward us, oblivious to their audience. The woman stared lovingly into the man's face. They spun around and around, hovering over the tracks. Mark and I couldn't believe what we were seeing. He managed to whisper to me, "Do you see that?" I said I did and we quietly started walking away. We were both very shaken, but curious as to who the ghosts were and what they were doing there.

As young people often do, we foolishly came back the next night, this time with my little sister, Ann. I was convinced that we hadn't seen anything, that indeed it had been a prank, and I was out to prove it. Mark had brought a flashlight, so he could shine it on the people's faces and call them on their prank. We sat on the bridge for a few hours, looking around nervously.

As time went on, we were convinced the encounter we had had the night before was really our eyes playing tricks on us. My sister Ann is a very down-to-earth person and she didn't believe that we had seen anything. She was truly the biggest skeptic sitting on the bridge that night.

We started to think our encounter was an illusion and decided to leave. Then, around midnight, we got the scare of our lives. From what I've heard of ghosts, they can't harm people. Sometimes they aren't even aware of people around. But this one was. Off near the trees, we saw that same faint light again that grew bigger as it got closer.

From the bottom of her dress, the ghost began to take form before our eyes as she walked toward us menacingly. There was a sense of anger in the air, like she didn't want us there and was going to make sure we left. Mark managed to lift up the flashlight and it went straight through her. We knew then this was not a prank. We felt like we were frozen for a second, then jumping up, we dashed down the railroad tracks and never looked back.

I have speculated on why she was angry and I wonder if the night before she had seen us watching her and her love dance the night away. I have often wondered if perhaps the couple had been killed in the woods or the woods were their secret meeting place. From the clothing they had been wearing, I guessed they had lived back in the 1700s or 1800s, a time when life was more proper and there were rules to be followed. The woods were the perfect place for a young couple to spend time together without being watched over by overprotective parents. Or if they had met a more sinister fate, that would explain the female ghost's anger. The one thing that was still puzzling to me was why she came after us the second night. The first night, we had watched them dancing, but left soon after. The second night, she was angry and came after us.

All I know is, we never went back to that bridge. We didn't want to risk the wrath of an angry entity, whether she could hurt us or not. Her scaring us was enough! We decided some things are better left alone.

Ohio-based freelance writer Diane Schmidt specializes in copywriting, articles, and editing. She has a BA in Communication-Journalism from Marist College and a background in marketing, Internet research, and graphic design. She is also owner and editor of Savingsmania.com a web site dedicated to helping people save money.

The Kiss

by Alex Porter
Stirling, Scotland

It happened in the spring of 1996. For a few minutes one afternoon my view of the world was ambushed by a reality that I had heard others talk about but had given little credence to. For that small segment of time I was visited by something that, even now, I am at a loss to fully explain.

There were nine of us; three teachers and six pupils from central Scotland off to the Ardennes forest in northern France. The pupils were aged between twelve and fifteen and were going to France to complete their gold and silver badges in map reading and outdoor orientation. Myself and the other teachers, Anne and Bill, were there to ensure safety and to check that the kids completed their tasks.

We left home in our crowded minibus on a cool Thursday evening and drove south overnight with me at the wheel. Our destination was a small village outside the town of Charleville-Mezieres, which lay just south of the Belgian border. We were booked into a hostel that had once served as a church. At five o'clock the next afternoon, hot and weary, we fell out of the bus in a jumble of empty soda cans, sandwich wraps, and music cassettes and found ourselves squinting through the strong, late afternoon sunlight at a curious two-story hybrid of a building.

The rear of the hostel had retained the outward appearance of being a church; arched windows, some still holding lozenges of coloured glass like captured flame, were set into ancient stonework long darkened by time. In complete contrast, the middle and front were all red-brick modernity. The curious thing was that the point where old met new was not marked by an even vertical line, but rather by a line as arbitrary as an earthquake fissure going diagonally from top to bottom. The result was that the first floor incorporated more of the old church than the ground floor. The entire structure resembled a garbled architecture put together by an idiot on speed!

We were welcomed by the manager, Marcel, and shown to our rooms on the first floor. I freshened up and then went downstairs to help unload the minibus. What I really wanted to do was sleep but I knew that we had to do some planning for the field trip the next day. I put it down to fatigue and being in a new environment. From the moment I had set foot in the building, I had felt a vague unease, a sense of something not being as it should. I could not explain it; it was simply there. Soon after we were sitting down to the evening meal. The kids chatted excitedly about the tasks facing them next day. As darkness fell we trudged upstairs to our beds.

Next morning I woke to the noise of bustling preparation. Kids called to each other along the corridor and, from the rooms on either side of me, came the sound of running water indicating that Anne and Bill were already up and raring to go. I jumped out of bed and started to dress. After a few minutes, however, an overwhelming lethargy took hold of me. My limbs felt as if they were being weighed down and my head throbbed with a dull pain like a displaced toothache. I sat down on the edge of the bed and tried to recover. After a couple of minutes I began to feel better and I finished getting dressed. I was relieved because the sun streaming through the window held the promise of a good day; a day for being on the hills.

By the time I had walked along the corridor and started to descend the stairs I knew that my relief was premature. I don't think I had ever felt as tired as I did at that moment. Strangely, I had the curious and unnerving sensation of being affected not by some inner malaise but by something external to my being, as if all the energy in my body was being siphoned off. My heart began beating loudly in my chest. I made it down to the dining room but I was sweating and the heaviness in my legs threatened to pull me to the floor. I remember, by an act of sheer will, forcing myself into some semblance of control. I rationalized; I was a fit young man who had just slept very deeply for over nine hours. I told myself that there was no reason why I should feel this way so I was going to pull myself together. It didn't work.

As I sat down at the breakfast table I knew that I would be in no fit state to go walking in the hills. It was Anne who came to my rescue.

"You look washed out," she said, concern plainly etched on her face. "Perhaps you should rest today." I could have hugged her! I mumbled something about having a stomach upset and this seemed to satisfy everyone. Leaving them to finish breakfast, I returned to my room, undressed, and was asleep before my head had warmed the pillow.

It must have been around noon when I woke. I felt refreshed.

I got up and went to the bathroom. On my return I opened the curtains. Sunlight flooded the room. I remember opening the window and then standing for some minutes to breathe in the fresh, spring-scented air. I felt good. The sluggish fatigue I had felt earlier was now replaced by a pleasant languor. Since I wasn't going anywhere I decided to return to bed and enjoy this new feeling of relaxation.

Even now, years later, I am not certain exactly when it started.

I remember studying the play of sunlight on the wall, then closing my eyes. Even the birds outside had gone silent. I felt at peace. I may have begun to doze but I am not sure. Then, very slowly, like a tide coming in, I became aware of a strange feeling of unease taking hold of me. At first I thought it was my sickness returning but soon realized that what I was feeling was more puzzling; I wanted to open my eyes but some inner voice insisted I keep them shut tight! I began to recognize what was happening to me — this was fear; I was slowly being overtaken by a feeling of growing dread that had no apparent cause.

Suddenly I found myself pitched into what I can only describe as a tug-of-war — and one I knew with a total intuitive conviction threatened my very life. It was as if two strong hands had taken hold of the bed covers and were attempting to pull them from me. I gripped onto them for all I was worth. The force countering me was immense. It took all of my strength to hang on and stop the blankets being torn from my grasp. All the time that inner voice was begging me to hang on, telling me that to lose this struggle was to enter a world of even worse terror — perhaps death itself.

I wanted to open my eyes, to face my tormentor, yet I knew, with equal force, that to do so would be to confront a horror I would not be able to withstand. I wanted to shout, to scream for help, but fear stopped up my mouth. I was trapped in this struggle and could not escape. I held on desperately but knew I was weakening. The hands — if they were hands— would not relent; slowly I felt the covers slipping from my grip. I was lost. I was like a shipwrecked sailor trying to hold on to the keel of an upturned boat but slowly slipping off.

Then, blessedly, the struggle ceased. My "opponent" had given up.

The fear was still present, still powerful, but I knew the worst was past. I wanted to open my eyes. I needed to check that the world had righted itself. Still, that inner guide said no. I obeyed.

Then it happened. On my forehead, still damp with sweat, I felt a warm kiss — a warm, moist kiss. It lasted only a second but even now I can recall the sensation. It was, unmistakably, a kiss and it liberated me from the terror I had felt. Suddenly I was filled with a serenity that was beyond the power of mere words to describe.

I turned onto my side and opened my eyes — just in time to catch a fleeting glimpse of a black shoe, a stockinged leg, and the hem of an ankle-length blue skirt disappearing out the door.

I sat up in shocked amazement. What was going on? Was I hallucinating? Was I the object of some elaborate Gallic practical joke? I dressed quickly and hurried downstairs. I collared Marcel at the reception desk and told him what had happened. I demanded to know who else was in the hostel. He assured me that the only other person in the hostel was the cook who was over sixty, was not wearing an ankle-length blue skirt, and had not recently come down the stairs.

I was about to make an embarrassed retreat when Marcel asked me to follow him. We walked the short distance to the corridor outside his office. The light there was bad so he switched on the ceiling light. On the wall were two photographs — one from WW II showing two rows of smiling GIs who were clearly recuperating from their wounds and the other, from WW I, with British wounded in the same pose, but with the set, grim expressions of those who had seen and been marked by much suffering.

Marcel explained that the church had served as a casualty station in both wars. It had been converted into two levels during 1915 and further modified the following year to incorporate single rooms for officers. Depending on the ebb and flow of battle, the station had sheltered British, French, German, and American casualties. At times, when the conflict had been at its height, the station was overwhelmed with wounded and quick decisions had to be made about those likely to survive and those not.

Marcel described reading once about dying soldiers being unceremoniously removed from their beds to make way for those who could be saved. They were usually taken to a row of tents placed in a field by the cemetery. Some, knowing what their displacement meant, clung to their blankets like men possessed.

He told me that my experience had happened to an American backpacker a decade before. That young man had vacated his room immediately. I could not blame him.

Before switching off the light Marcel drew my attention to the photographs. At the end of each row of soldiers was a nurse.

Each nurse was dressed in the same outfit — starched white aprons and caps, black shoes, and... ankle-length blue skirts!

I live in central Scotland about thirty miles from Edinburgh. My town was the background for the film *Braveheart*.

I am married with three children. My wife, Annice, is a technical officer involved in building and architecture.

Until two years ago I was a teacher of religious studies and philosophy. A heart attack ended my career. Now I write as much as I can and spend a lot of time reading and walking. I am also interested in spiritual healing.

I have had a few poems and articles published in the small press and hope to continue to learn to improve my craft. I would be happy to talk to anyone about my experience in France or about writing in general. My email is redeck12@aol.com.

The Hotel Room Guest

by Robin Lofton
Hawaii, United States

It has been said that London is the most haunted city in the world. Whether the veracity of this statement can be proven is not the subject of my story. But one thing I can say with conviction: ghosts abound in this tale of one city. From the Tower of London where the "rich and famous" were ceremoniously beheaded to London's still poverty-stricken East End, which many say has not changed since the 1888 murderous rampage of Jack the Ripper, London has a mixed history of high civilization, squalor, and untimely death. Poe himself could not have created a better setting for a haunting! My haunted encounter shows that ghosts continue to live in this city of Dickens, beer, and fish-'n-chips. In fact, they sometimes like to stay in hotels….

It happened three years ago while I was visiting my father who had, after more than thirty years of practicing law, decided to do the unthinkable: return to school. And London was his city of choice. I was living in Europe at the time, so I decided to visit him. Actually, I was worried about him — arriving in this strange city in the dead of night with only a suitcase and lacking any sense of direction. Well, I figured he had spent enough years worrying about me as a child, now it was my turn to worry about him. I made up some excuse about needing to research my book at a law library and took off for London. Never did I anticipate my otherworldly encounter!

But I'm getting ahead of myself. I chose a large but modest hotel on Russell Square — a place famous for its schools, libraries, and, of course, pubs. Convincing my father to stay at the hotel with me was not a difficult task, particularly since I made him an irresistible offer: a comfortable room with an English breakfast and cable television. We spent several days exploring London and, to keep up my ruse, several law libraries. Since I had lived in London a few years earlier, I showed him the touristy hangouts on Oxford and Bond streets as well as the not-so-touristy antique bookstores and ethnic restaurants. The roles were truly reversed! I was the leader; he the follower. And after several days of this *Freaky Friday*-style living, we both were ready to call it quits.

By the last day of my visit, my father had seen just about all of the London that he wanted to experience. He resigned himself to staying in the room, watching his favorite show: CNBC. I was still shopping and exploring, an experience I enjoyed even more since I wasn't dragging my reluctant non-tourist with me. Late in the afternoon, I returned to the room; we had agreed to meet there and then find a place for dinner. As I stepped off the elevator, I could hear CNBC blasting in the hallway.

"Good. He's already here," I thought, both gratefully and ominously. I'd had a very productive shopping day and was carrying an armload of bags. I had not yet started to worry about how I was going to pack all my goodies for my return trip. My immediate concern was that my room key was in my purse, probably at the bottom where it always worked its way to, and I didn't feel like looking for it.

"No problem. I'll just knock on the door," I thought. I could hear the familiar CNBC voices blasting on the television so I *knew* that my father was in the room waiting for me. I knocked politely and waited.

And I waited.

I knocked harder, but still politely. And waited. And waited. Still no answer.

I began to get annoyed. I banged hard on the door, causing it to jiggle on its hinges. I had lost my sense of politeness by this time.

He must hear this, I thought to myself. Again, I waited. And waited. I continued to hold all my shopping bags while I stood in front of the door, waiting to be let into the room.

I could clearly hear the voices on the television. They discussed various companies and the day's performance of the European markets. Still, I waited. I really did not relish the idea of digging into my disorganized, overstuffed purse to find my room key.

"Anyway, he's just sitting there! But he'll just have to get up and open the door!" I said aloud to myself. I banged on the door again. And waited.

The DAX. The FTSE. The New York Stock Exchange. The NASDAQ. I listened. And I waited. Finally, deciding to take some initiative, I stabilized my shopping bags in one hand and started digging in my purse for the room key. My annoyance was increasing to a dangerously high level. I began muttering about how *he's probably going to open the door just as I find the room key.* Then, I found it. But still no Father.

I pushed the room key into the door, waited for the green light, and pulled — actually, I ripped — it out. Then pushed open the door.

It happened in an instant. I saw and heard CNBC on the television. I caught a quick glimpse of a news reporter; viewed the ticker tape going slowly across the bottom of the screen; glimpsed the currency figures in the bottom right corner. Everything that I had expected — the collage of colors, numbers, and people flashing on the active television screen. But only for a quick second. Then it turned off.

I hurriedly looked at the bed, expecting to see my father sleeping there. But he wasn't. He wasn't in the room at all.

I was the only person in the room. Or was I?

The room and the hallway suddenly felt eerily silent. No television sounds. No banging on the door. No voice calling. The television screen was dark. The room was dead quiet. What was happening here? Just like seeing something move in the corner of your eye and turning your head quickly toward it but finding nothing, I felt that I had seen something but perhaps I did not. Was my imagination out of control?

They still say that London is the most haunted city in the world. Perhaps they're right. At least the hotel did not charge me for having an extra guest!

Robin Lofton has truly experienced life in many worlds! A native of northern California, she has lived in the Netherlands, where she obtained an advanced legal degree; England, where she experienced her haunted encounter; Sweden, where she braved freezing temperatures and dark days; and finally Belgium, where she has indulged her chocolate obsession. After working as a human rights attorney, adjunct professor of law and English, meditation coach, editor, options trader, and fruitcake vendor, Robin's vision turned to her first love: writing. A long-time practitioner of meditation, she teaches meditation through her fiction stories to attorneys, nurses, stock traders, parents, and other overworked, overstressed persons. Her "meditational fiction" stories are designed to quickly empower busy people with useful meditation practices and techniques to relieve stress and promote wellness — in one hour or less! Never one to be limited, Robin has also published articles on living in Sweden and Belgium, promoting international human rights law around the world, and trading stocks and options. Robin resides in Belgium with her hardworking husband and hard-playing infant son. She enjoys hearing from other avid readers and meditation addicts. She can be contacted at rlofton@earthlink.net.

Le Chesnay

by S. Faunières
Ontario, Canada

Many of us do not like sleeping in the house. At night, we find it difficult to breathe. As we lie in our beds, it feels as though a weight sits on our chests, making our breathing laboured and difficult. My cousin, who suffers from asthma, has become convinced that he suffers a deathly allergy in the house and refuses to sleep there.

When we sleep in the children's room, my grandfather's old office, the feeling grows in intensity. When the shutters close on that room and the thick curtains blot out the remaining light, the room becomes uncomfortably dark. I would call it deathly dark. The room has a narrow, rectangular shape and the resemblance it bears to an overgrown coffin makes me shudder nearly every night I sleep in there.

I used to avoid the room until he started talking to me. I slept in other rooms, where the light of the moon could find its way in either through a round, shutterless window or through a slit in the curtains. He would still find me, squeezing the air out of my lungs, but the feeling would disappear when I set my eyes on a ray of light seeping through. Some nights in the children's room, the coffin room, particularly in the fall and winter, the suffocating feeling has such depth that I must draw the curtains open, open the window, open the shutters, and sit on the window ledge to catch my breath.

He did not die in this room. He died on the main floor. He searches for his little sister, although he knows that she died before he did. She died in the mountains of Auvergne during World War I from food poisoning. She ate bad grapes that had grown and grow still in her aunt and uncle's vineyard. He misses her. He feels that he should have either died with her in Auvergne or saved her from her fate. But his illness had prevented him from travelling to safety to Auvergne. He had stayed in Normandy on the doctor's orders, in the company of a nurse. Perhaps if his mother had not run away things might have turned out differently.

When the war ended, his father returned and remarried. They had a daughter — my grandmother.

The boy became a teenager. He had no social outlet. The doctor prescribed sunbathing to heal him of his skin ailment. Leprosy. To a boy who desperately wanted to fit in, to blend in with others, the disease held a horrifying stigma.

He retreated further and further into himself. The adults in the household seemed more concerned with his new half-sister than with him. He did not find her the least bit interesting. He wanted his other sister back, the one who had understood him. He wanted her back. He wanted his mother. Why did his mother not return?

The boy's father, sensing his son's despair, tried not to leave him alone in the house. The housekeeper walked my grandmother to school one day in spite of strict instructions from the master of the house that the boy have someone with him at all times. Before the housekeeper came back to the house, the boy had found his father's hunting gun. He had loaded it with shells and retreated to the bedroom next to the kitchen. His father's bedroom. Awkwardly, he held the shotgun toward himself. The barrel was longer than his arm. Still, he managed, using his toes, to pull the trigger so that the shot exploded through his upper chest, just below his right shoulder. The diseased shoulder. He did not die right away. He coughed blood for some time before he choked and died, minutes before the housekeeper returned to the house.

They kept his body for a short time, for the wake. They could not invite anyone though, for the boy had committed suicide, a sin for a Catholic family. This did not prevent his father from grieving. He had loved the boy very much.

They put the body in a casket and moved it to the second floor. Not the most convenient spot, certainly, but they could not very well leave it in the main floor bedroom, covered as it was with blood and flesh — not to mention the shotgun pellets imbedded in the back wall. The boy's stepmother insisted that they keep the body away from the room she shared with her daughter. So they placed the casket in the narrow, rectangular room upstairs. There the boy's father prayed for his son's lost soul for a few days before the cart came to take the body and the casket to the pauper's cemetery. They could not bury the boy in the church cemetery for, according to the church, victims of suicide and leprosy did not belong in hallowed grounds.

Much as he had wanted escape, and perhaps this proved the church dictates true, the boy's spirit remained in the house. He saw his father praying and wondered why his spirit still lingered in the house. *Why did he not see his sister? Where had she gone?* He no longer had a shape, no longer had a voice. He longed to ask someone *why* but no one could hear him.

He wandered in the house for years. Often the house lay empty with no one but the flies to feel his presence. Other times our family came. We all have felt his weight bearing down on our chests in the dark of the night. Some, like my cousin, thought that the cause of our breathlessness hailed from allergies.

Others, like my grandmother, think that the darkness of the night gives us a feeling of oppression. She recommends opening the curtains to let some light through. My aunt thinks that with the curtains, windows, and shutters closed, the house lacks air. According to her, opening windows helps. I know that when we get up from our beds, he can no longer show us that he seeks a way out.

When I visit the house, I feel him welcome me back but I do not consider myself a very good friend to him. I can only listen to him. I can also call him to me when he tries to get someone else's attention. But I cannot show him the way home to the light. I wish I could, for his sadness and loss lay heavy in my heart.

S. Faunières now lives in Barrie, Ontario. Barrie is described as a city with moderate weather, something S. Faunières regards as something of a lie. Snow accumulations amount to eight or nine feet every winter and temperatures frequently dip below 20 degrees Celsius. She and her husband have three very lively, busy children. She teaches French as a second language at the local college and writes in her spare time. S. Faunières has completed a full-length novel and is in the process of finishing a second one. Neither manuscript has found a home with a publisher or an agent yet but she is actively working on remedying the situation.

The Poltergeist

by Lisa Wetzmuller
Peterborough, England

I never believed in ghosts, and I used to laugh at my friends when they told me stories of supernatural encounters that they had had. All that changed the summer we rented an old house by the sea in Italy. It was a lovely Mediterranean bungalow, perched upon a hill and overlooking an azure bay. The huge wild garden was full of fruit trees, flowers, bushes, and palm trees, and to me, it resembled a small Eden. I could not understand why its owners did not want to live there anymore — everything about it seemed so perfect.

Our party consisted of me, one of my girlfriends, and two befriended couples. Since there were only three bedrooms in the house, my friend Lily and I decided to share one of the bedrooms. We had brought a portable radio with us, which we set up and turned on immediately after we had arrived, to get us into a party mood while we were unpacking. I was just humming to a favorite tune and moving into the bathroom to unpack my toiletries, when the music suddenly stopped.

"Hey, what's going on?" I yelled to Lily, who was folding her clothes in the bedroom. "I really liked that song, why did you turn it off?"

"I didn't." Lily's surprised face appeared in the doorway. "It must have turned itself off; I wasn't even close to the radio!"

"Impossible," I said, moving toward the offending boom box in order to examine it. "Radios don't just turn themselves off.

There must be an explanation. Is the power in the house still on?"

Lily flicked a light switch. "Yep, all working."

"Hmm." Bending over the radio, I saw that the on/off switch had been slid to the side, into the "off" position. I turned the radio back on — music blasted forth just as before.

"Strange," I shook my head in disbelief. "Perhaps there's something wrong with the radio, though I've never had that problem before." I shot a suspicious glance at Lily, who innocently continued unpacking. Was she making fun of me by pretending that it hadn't been her joke?

When the radio turned itself off for the second time, we were both in the room and reading. Neither of us was close to the radio. But suddenly, the power switch flicked into the "off" position again. We looked at each other in disbelief, but said nothing. Over the next few days, the same thing kept happening several times a day. Sometimes the radio turned itself on; sometimes it switched to "off." These occurrences only happened when either Lily or I were in the room. None of our other friends ever witnessed the uncanny spectacle, though we had told them about it and were eager for them to believe us.

It was Oliver who first suggested that it might be a poltergeist. As he explained, poltergeists are mischievous spirits that can haunt houses or people by moving objects, making noises, or even assaulting persons. He said that poltergeists were not usually malevolent but that they enjoyed frightening and annoying people, and that the best way to deal with them was to talk strictly to them, as to a child or dog. Of course, I wasn't having any of that nonsense. As a total rationalist, I was sure that there must be a more plausible explanation for what was going on. Also, as I pointed out, a dodgy radio alone was not enough evidence for any kind of ghost, let alone a poltergeist.

But stranger things began to happen over the next few days. One morning, when I woke up, my wristwatch was gone. I was sure that I had placed it on the bedside table the previous evening, the way I always do. When I told Lily, she made some jokes about me having had too much of the Italian pinot grigio the night before, and suggested I should have a look in the bathroom.

I searched not only the bathroom but the whole house — nothing. Our friends remembered me wearing the watch the day before, but nobody had seen it since or could remember me taking it off. As it was quite an expensive watch, I became very upset when I realized that it was probably lost for good — everybody had helped to look, with no results.

Around lunchtime I felt exhausted, so I decided to just stretch out on the bed and try to relax for a little while. When I stepped into the bedroom, the first thing that caught my eye was my wristwatch — lying in the center of the bedside table! I had cleared and searched the bedside table many times in the course of the morning, and the watch hadn't been there. For a moment, I suspected that Lily might have pulled a sick joke on me, but when she entered the room and I saw her utterly surprised face, I knew she hadn't taken it. The incident remained unexplained.

Another time, when we were getting ready for bed, I noticed that Lily had draped her straw hat over the glass lampshade on the table, but had forgotten to turn the light off. Worried that the hat might burn, I switched the lamp off and joined Lily in the bathroom.

Only a few minutes later, Lily crinkled her nose, "Is that a burned smell in here?"

"Yeah, funny," I replied, "it seems to come from the bedroom. I'll have a look." I rushed back into the bedroom and discovered that Lily's straw hat was smoking on top of the lighted lamp, almost completely black already. A few minutes longer and I am sure it would have burst into flames.

This was not the end of our strange experiences. One early morning, the wooden shutters of the French windows leading out to the garden from our room started rattling like crazy, though there was absolutely no breeze. It was almost as if somebody was standing outside, banging the doors in an attempt to force them open and to get into our room. Despite my terror, I forced myself to get up and open the shutters, in case it might be an animal. But when I looked, I saw and heard nothing. The noise stopped, and even after I had gone back to bed, the shutters remained firmly closed.

Another day, as I was laying the dinner table, a wine glass suddenly crashed to the floor and broke, though I had been nowhere near it and certainly hadn't touched it. Lily found one of her T-shirts torn in the cupboard. Several pages were ripped out of one of my favorite novels. The laces of one of my trainers disappeared for a while, only to be found among the oleander in the garden.

Strangely enough, nothing ever happened to our friends. It seemed as if Lily and I were the chosen victims of some invisible prankster, making us seem like loonies to the rest of the party, who saw no evidence of ghosts except a torn book and some broken glasses.

Only Oliver believed us and, following his advice, we secretly began to speak to the poltergeist, asking it to do us no harm, as we were only temporary visitors in the house. Unfortunately, our long speeches had little effect. Things continued to be lost or destroyed without Lily or me even being near them. It began to dawn on me that the landlords might have a good reason for not wanting to stay in the house anymore. Perhaps the poltergeist was one of theirs, a relative who had died in the house and not found rest. When we got back from our holiday, I even contacted the owners of the house and asked them about the strange occurrences, but they claimed never to have noticed anything. Also, the eerie happenings stopped as soon as we were back home. We never went back to the haunted holiday house, and we never got to the bottom of the secret it harbored.

I grew up in Austria, in the beautiful Tyrolean Alps. After graduating from high school in Vienna, I was eager to explore some sunnier climes, and so I applied to the University of California, Santa Barbara. To my own great surprise, I was accepted, and four years later I graduated from Santa Barbara with a BA in Comparative Literature.

By then keen to get back to bad old Europe, I applied to the University of Edinburgh in Scotland next, from where I have got a Master's Degree in English Literature. After a short traineeship for a publisher of art books in London, I am now doing my best to earn a living as a freelance writer, tutor, and researcher. I have always been full of stories and ideas, and by writing full time I am fulfilling a lifelong dream.

Apart from writing, I am also a fanatic dog owner and horse rider. For me, there is nothing more relaxing than to be out and about with my lab or horse, preferably both at the same time. I love hiking, too, and on the weekends my boyfriend, the dog, and I are often seen rambling in the local countryside. With all the fog we get here, I am sure people sometimes mistake us for ghosts as well!

Rose

by Jo Franklin
Berkshire, United Kingdom

Perhaps, because my job is working in an old museum, I had become more sensitive to echoes from the past. Something about the place — the long corridors lined with dusty books — induces ghostly thoughts. I had been there for quite some time, working in rather bizarre conditions, and had come to accept these feelings by rationalizing them.

We always said that when a book moved, unseen, from one shelf to another, it was something to do with someone not reshelving it properly rather than anything supernatural. We accepted the fact that sometimes doors suddenly wouldn't open by declaring that it was due to the slow collapse of the whole improperly built structure; it had been a portacabin constructed in the 1960s, as a temporary replacement building for the museum, and was sinking under the weight of mountains of archives on the bending floors.

We accepted the strange garden with its wild flowers and its dilapidated old building, now an outstore, which was reported to have been part of a military camp and used as a cinema for the soldiers during the Second World War.

No one batted an eyelid at the nettles and the butterflies, the foxes that crept from underneath the building, and the occasional rat or mouse that came to visit. All was part of the scene we worked in, some of it dating back to the late 1930s. Anyway, we were soon to move. To go to a grand and important house, which would turn us into something magnificent and worth visiting, if only for the fine period house itself.

And so it was on that sunny morning in June — not the sort of day when you might be disturbed by ghosts or strange energies — that I sat at my desk, a pile of old books in front of me. As with all book donations, each book had to be carefully referenced, written into a register and then into a computer database. Each one I processed quite leisurely. They were interesting, partly for the fact that they were given to us by someone who had chanced upon them in a box in their garage. They were varied books, published at different times in the last century, historical records.

I worked steadily through them until... concealed in one of the books was a letter written in June 1942 by someone called Rose, to her Jack. It was a beautiful letter — a love letter, containing exquisite words of endearment and affection. Letters like this would have been only too common during those dark days of the war. It talked of her love for him, and how she longed for the days when he would be back, and they could go to the camp picture house once more, take walks in the country, and it spoke of all the other wonderful things they could do together.

It was written in pen, and the last few words were smudged, perhaps by tears from the writer. As I held the letter carefully in my hands I swear I could smell the faint aroma of a perfume, one that reminded me of roses in the garden. Roses from a Rose. Had the young serviceman ever received the letter? Rather curious, I lay the letter and book to one side, hoping, as soon as my busy work schedule allowed, to find out more.

Maybe it was the air of beauty about the letter that made me want to keep it within reach — just for this, my moment in time. Something had come into my hands that spelled out a precious feeling between two young people, threatened by the clouds of the war. For whatever reason, I wanted to enjoy its closeness.

Perhaps later I should really leave it quietly secreted in the book, back in the shelves, not to resurface for another fifty years or so, or even longer — was this why it had been placed there in the first instant?

The weather was warm. We always took our coffee breaks outside if we possibly could — sandwiched between the crumbling old portacabin and the equally crumbling old outstore. We delighted in each other's company, merrily chatting and savouring the delights of the wildness of our so-called garden. Reluctant to leave one day, I lingered on in the sunlight after the others had gone. The sun warmed me. After a while I knew I had to go back in.

But suddenly I heard a noise from the outstore. I wheeled round. There was nothing to be seen. The outstore door remained firmly closed; the small paned windows, some of them cracked, were too dirty to see through. And yet I could have sworn I heard a giggle from the inside. I hesitated — could it be one of the staff? No, surely not. Curiosity drove me on. I got out a key and checked the door but it was securely locked, so I felt sure that no one was inside. I started to walk away. I had not reached the main building when I heard the outstore door opening! Once again I wheeled around, expecting a rational explanation, perhaps a familiar face, but I saw no one. But something came out. There was a light tripping of feet on the stone path, a drift of rose perfume in the air, an almost inaudible laugh. Something brushed past me, and the door of the old picture house closed quietly.

"Rose? Jack?" I whispered.

Silence.

I wandered back inside, quite bemused, and sat at my desk. Imagination? Too much sun? Too much chatting and banter at the coffee break? Who knows.

And yet when I tried to find the letter from Rose… I couldn't. I searched through all the books on my desk and in my office. But to no avail. Like the lovers, it had disappeared.

Taken by a member of staff?

Or taken by the lovers?

Jo Franklin has written many short stories on such subjects as crime, science fiction, and romance. Recently she was pleased to win awards and get published in U.K.'s prestigious *Writing Magazine* — first prize in the Science Fiction Short Story 2002/03 competition, and first prize in the Crime Short Story 2003/04 competition. Jo has also written three novels. The latest, *Cytherea's Island*, is a tale of horror and fantasy.

She has always felt that she has a sixth sense. As a little girl she had ghostly experiences when living in a big old house; flowers got thrown around and she felt she was being observed. On holiday in an old cottage in Norfolk she saw an apparition — a tall man dressed in a fisherman's jersey. And working in an old museum has not eased things — doors opening and closing and locking themselves, and presences from the past being sensed, like Rose and Jack in "Rose."

Jo lives in leafy Berkshire, England, with her grey cat Tigger, and her partner, Roger.

The Weeping Man in the Sunshine

by Ann Howard
Sydney, Australia

When I came to Australia from England, the first impression I had was of blue skies and brilliant sunshine. It does rain here, of course, but the weather is mostly like high summer, so different from England, and just not the sort of place you'd think of seeing ghosts.

I now know that ghosts do not wait for pitch-black nights or grey evenings to appear to us.

We moved to Sydney and soon after our small family had settled in, I went back to work as a teacher in a nearby college. The college building was near a very busy highway, with nonstop traffic. I chose to take a train to the closest station and walk to the college for exercise. It was a fairly long walk, about fifteen minutes, and I didn't enjoy walking alongside the dusty highway with its fumes and noise, so I looked for an alternative route.

There was an adjoining hospital and a park, and I explored the grounds. They linked up, and I was pleased to see there were no fences. As I walked through the park, the birds were singing and the trees rustling in a soft breeze. The traffic seemed a long way away. At the edge of the park was a small cemetery.

Now, I have always enjoyed walking through cemeteries and reading old gravestone inscriptions as I am a bit of a history buff. Australia, like many other colonized places, has a dramatic history which can be illuminated by the stories that gravestones tell. Early colonizers had large families but often little children sadly died because of bad drinking water and lack of medicines. If they survived their childhood, they often lived well into their nineties.

One particular morning, I had plenty of time before my class and my teaching notes and marking were all completed, so I sauntered through the cemetery in the hot sunshine, reading about Martha and Eliza and Gilbert and William and wondering about their lives so long ago.

Suddenly, I clutched my briefcase to my chest in absolute terror. A man dressed in old-fashioned clothes — breeches with an elaborate hat and wig — was kneeling on one knee at a small grave and weeping silently. He was clearly visible, but a silvery shining grey, with no color in his face or clothes. The sun shone on large silver tears falling from his eyes and through his transparent face.

I have never experienced an emotion like the fear I had at that moment — my eyes widened, the back of my neck prickled, I felt sick and dizzy, and I felt my jaw drop. As if sensing my panic, the weeping man turned and looked full at me. I felt strongly he had an unbearable burden to carry and was looking for someone to take it from him. He gestured to me and started to rise. I was so terrified I dropped my case, which had everything in it, and ran like the wind, faster than I have ever run, blindly in a line away from the weeping man, toward the college. The sound of the traffic now seemed friendly but too far away. The sun glinted on the closed windows of the college which also seemed so far away and blind to my distress. I was alone in a cemetery with a deranged ghost!

My feet pounded up the immaculate grass path toward the college. I longed to see someone — anyone — but except for the hum of cars in the distance, I could have been alone in the world. I did not dare to look over my shoulder but the air was full of menace. I choked, sobbed, and pulled air into my lungs as I ran.

When I stood panting at the road in front of the college park, the fear dropped from me like a cloak. I felt so foolish — a middle-aged woman dropping her briefcase in the middle of a sunny afternoon and running for her life. I saw two of my students, Karl and Jacob, and called out to them.

"Coming to class, miss?" Karl called.

"I have to walk back — must have left my briefcase in the little cemetery when I knelt to look at an inscription," I lied.

"We'll walk back with you to find it," Jacob said with a smile.

Inwardly, I breathed a sigh of relief. This is what I hoped they'd say.

"Your essays are in that case — I've marked them."

"We might change our minds, then," joked Karl, and we retraced my steps, the two tall students reassuringly on either side of me.

I felt jumpy. Some of the headstones were really large and the apparition could be hiding behind them, staring with those agonized silvery eyes.

"It's a bit creepy in here," Karl muttered.

"Rubbish!" Jacob smashed his right fist into his left hand. He had trained for the Olympic Games and was heavily muscled. It was comforting to have his big presence.

We reached the spot where I had seen the weeping man. There was my briefcase, and there, next to the gravestone, the grass was darker green and flattened as though someone or something had been kneeling there.

The three of us stared at the mossy headstone. An inscription read:

Sacred to the memory of Mary Olver, daughter of Luke and Margerey Olver, late of this Parish. She died as a result of an accident on the 13th day of November, in the Year of our Lord 1833, aged seven years. Safe in the arms of Jesus.

Karl shivered. "Class starts in five minutes," he said. Karl had a fine-boned face and long fingers.

I thought about the weeping man often after that morning. Was he the little girl's father? Did he cause her death? Why was he looking so guilty?

I stopped catching the train and walking and drove right up to the college car park every day. When I was pacing up and down in front of my class, I would gaze down from the college windows at the cemetery, half expecting to see the silvery weeping man gazing up at me, his eyes pleading for some relief from his burden. I never walked through the cemetery again.

A few months passed. I gave the class an essay to write with the title "A Strange Experience." The essays were adequate, but not very exciting and I sat marking them in my apartment, yawning and wanting to switch on the TV.

I came to the last essay. It was Karl Zeit's — the same Karl who had walked back with me to find my briefcase. I flicked the pages to the last paragraph and the following words caught my eye:

> "...what is really so strange is that the other two people I was with could not see him... his hair and face were silvery and his eyes were awful. I would have been really scared but he was looking straight past me, his eyes fixed on the woman standing next to me. She was talking and laughing with my friend, Jacob, and did not seem to see the apparition at all."

Ann Howard is a grandmother who was born in England but lives in Australia. As you can see from her picture, she enjoys life but assures the reader that her ghost story is absolutely true. Ann is a frequently published fiction and historical nonfiction writer.

Spooked by Love

by Nan B. Clark
Massachusetts, United States

What would you do if you discovered your teenaged lover's family expected a ghost to choose his bride?

In the spring of 1968, the United States was at war not only overseas but on the home front as well. Armies of angry, often stoned young men and women swarmed through city streets in savage protest of the Vietnam mess with the cry, "Make love, not war." Perhaps our flowers-in-the-hair passion had been primitively stirred by the public shedding of blood, bringing murder itself into the home as if it were just another drama.

Television screens showed scenes of unspeakable horror not only in the jungles and deltas but in our own backyards with the shootings of Martin Luther King and Robert Kennedy.

Reacting to the sense of impending doom in the air, I became romantically involved with a student at an Ivy League college in northern New England. Daniel most zealously did not want to go to Vietnam. His fraternity brothers were turning to a number of ways to beat the system, some of them aiming for grad school, others planning to head to Canada, and still others taking what seemed the simplest way out and impregnating a girlfriend in hopes that that would put them out of reach of Uncle Sam's first line of fire as a family man with dependents.

As an eighteen-year-old sophomore at a women's college in southern Massachusetts, I knew I was nowhere near ready to make such a commitment. But my hormones disagreed. For my parents, the biggest horror in life would be to produce a daughter who "had to get married." The mixed message of those days was get a degree, but don't use it in real life. Get a husband, but don't do it by entrapment. Get smart, but look dumb. What was a girl to do — listen to her parents or her hormones?

Daniel thought I could support us both after he graduated, doing office work while he went to law school. I didn't want to type; I wanted to write. He said that of course I could write; I could do it at night, after the kids were asleep. I didn't think that would work, but was afraid to appear cold and selfish. I accepted his gold fraternity pin and pretended to dream of pink and blue bundles of joy.

That June I won a national poetry prize, then another. There was going to be a presentation ceremony at the Harvard Faculty Club in Cambridge, Massachusetts, and I was invited to give a reading. I received this information from my mother in Daniel's frat house, via the lone battered public phone booth buried in the basement. When I tried to share my exciting news over the roar of the keg party, I didn't make much of a dent in Daniel's consciousness, not even when I said I had to leave.

Back home in Manchester, New Hampshire, I got ready for my big night by buying a minidress with a frill at the neck huge enough for Elizabeth I, the Virgin Queen, and teal blue sling-backs. Smoking endless filtered cigarettes on a bus into Cambridge, I watched as a huge thunderstorm blackened the Boston skyline. It knocked out the electricity just as I stepped to the microphone but after a few weird flickering seconds, the power came back on. I delivered my poem, bowed to the applause, and felt well on the way to becoming the next Sylvia Plath, except for the part about sticking my head in the oven and dying young.

I didn't notice for a few days that I hadn't heard from Daniel. Then, I thought I could feel my heart breaking with each day of silence. Finally, about three weeks after the reading, I received a postcard from California. Daniel had "needed time to get his head together," to figure out what he was going to do his senior year. He realized that he missed me, loved me, and couldn't wait to see me. I tore the postcard to shreds. He called my parents' place in New Hampshire over and over again when he got back to Philadelphia. Finally, I invited him up, intending to dump him face to face. Instead, I ended up in the apple orchard flat on my back.

Daniel had no qualms whatsoever about what we'd done — having unprotected sex at a dangerous time of the month. It was time to meet his parents, to go to Philadelphia where they lived in a row house smelling of damp rot and lemons. They seemed to like me, at least better than they did the local draft board. Besides, Daniel's sister had just had a baby, and everybody was thrilled.

I agreed to ride back up north with his parents, who were on their way to visit friends in Maine, while Daniel stayed behind to earn a few paychecks pumping gas before going back to college. His mother and father and I would spend the night at the old family homestead in southwestern Connecticut, a farmhouse that had been in Daniel's father's family since the early 1700s.

We arrived in country darkness, unbroken except for the yellow rectangles of uncurtained windows gleaming out at us from the façade of the huge, colonial farmhouse. Inside, Daniel's aunt — her husband was his father's brother — several cousins, and what seemed like a dozen farm workers were sitting around an enormous table in the kitchen, eating peach pie that smelled like heaven and dripped with heavy cream.

Daniel's mother showed me around the rooms with their smoky beams, wide pine floorboards, and whitewashed walls, pointing out the little birthing room adjacent to the huge brick chimney and taking pains to point out what appeared to be ancient fingernail scratches in the plaster.

His aunt had put me in a small, lonely room at the top of the back staircase, which turned at a sharp angle to open onto a hallway. The massive chimney jutted out into the small room, barely leaving enough room for a single bed at a right angle to the open door. There were no curtains at the window, and no shade to pull. I undressed by moonlight and yanked on an old T-shirt, wondering if biology would soon force me to be part of this family.

As soon as I lay down in the little bed with its thin mattress supported by old ropes that creaked like the rigging of a ship every time I shifted, the footsteps started. I stared up at the plastered ceiling wondering what all those farmhands in the attic were doing. Crushing spiders? Square-dancing? Back and forth they went, click, click, click, to one side of the brick wall of the chimney looming at me, then click, click, click, past the foot of my bed to the open door and the hallway beyond with its opening onto the staircase.

I swung my legs over the side of the bed, opened my suitcase, and fished around for my cigarettes. A breeze drifted in through the window screen as I went to strike the match. With the cigarette in my mouth, I looked toward the doorway and felt a horrible shock run through me. Either his mother or his aunt had caught me in the act of smoking, and in bed, no less.

Frozen with horror, I stared at the dumpy female figure outlined in the dark doorway. Glints in the area of the face indicated spectacle lenses. A white cap concealed her hair. Two long, white ribbons trailed down the front of her shapeless black gown. She emanated a sense of severity, of judgment, of doom.

At first she was solid.

Then she was dematerializing.

Then she was gone altogether.

What kind of a crazy joke was Daniel's family playing?

Ripping the match across the rough swatch on the bottom of the matchbook, I lit up. Furiously I blew smoke through the window screen as I sucked on nicotine and outrage. After crushing out the butt in the empty fake gold compact I carried for just such occasions — not seeing ghosts, but sneaking cigarettes — I lay back and shut my eyes. The yokels overhead, obviously in cahoots with Daniel's family, could tango away the night for all I cared. They wouldn't get a rise out of me.

In the morning, I was the last one down for breakfast, kept awake for most of the night by the thought that some old bat — An ancient family retainer? A mad great-grand-aunt? — was spying on me. As I approached that huge table, Daniel's mother and his aunt asked how I had slept. Fine, I said. Like a baby. In fact, the only good part of the night had been when I got up out of bed to go to the bathroom and discovered I wasn't going to be a teenaged mother.

The telephone rang. His aunt answered it. It was for me. It was Daniel. The two women decided to bang out the kitchen screen door together. When I picked up the receiver, I started right in, telling him about the stupid joke. When I stopped to draw breath, he said, "They must be really happy that you saw her."

"I didn't tell anybody anything," I said smugly.

"Tell them, then," he said. "Tell them you saw her."

My heart jumped. "What are you talking about?"

They didn't know who she was, but she'd been appearing to young women who were about to marry into the family for as long as anyone could remember.

"Why didn't you mention this before?" I asked, bewildered by his apparent sincerity.

"Nobody believes in ghosts," he said. "And besides, what if I had told you and you hadn't seen her? Then how would you feel, rejected by the family spirit?"

I hung up, confused and suspicious. Had he been laughing at me? Were they all laughing at me? Why?

I went outside and found his mother and his aunt. I asked them if there was a matchmaking ghost in the house. They laughed sheepishly. Then they admitted they had both been put in that room before their marriages, and they had both seen something, or someone, an old woman, in fact, with granny glasses and a chillingly judgmental air.

Whatever else she was, the apparition in the hallway turned out to be far from clairvoyant. After trying to make sense of it all and getting no help from Daniel, who just repeated that I had been chosen by the family spirit, I gleefully dumped him that Christmas and have never been haunted once in all these years by even the faintest whisper of regret.

Nan B. Clark lives on the northern coast of Massachusetts in the city of Beverly, which was part of Salem until 1668. For many years she has worked for The Society for the Preservation of New England Antiquities, first teaching an eighteenth-century decorative technique called japanning in which the designs are three-dimensional and gilded, and then as a seasonal guide at Beauport, a forty-room mansion overlooking Gloucester Harbor. In 2002, her husband, Tom, produced her one-act play about President William Howard Taft's summer White House in Beverly as a fund-raiser to restore the nineteenth-century carriage house on the site. Tom is a direct descendant of Susannah Martin, one of the nineteen victims hanged during the Salem witchcraft trials of 1692.

Harry

by Dennis Walker
Oakham, Great Britain

Mention the word "ghost" to the average person and it conjures up a vision of an ethereal transparent creature seen only in conditions of mist or moonlight or in a place of supernatural repute. A being that makes an entrance or exit accompanied by the creaking of doors, although the more sophisticated of the species can simply walk through walls.

If you claim to have seen a ghost, you immediately become suspect as a person who was inebriated. This may be a justified suspicion as inns have a long tradition of being haunted and therefore people are half conditioned to encounter a spectral presence. A heavy meal also induces a period of semi-sleep in which the slightest creak on a stair may be misinterpreted. It may also be suggested that the person witnessing an apparition is suffering from an unsound mind, which is, of course, difficult to disprove.

My ghost was certainly not a floating figment of imagination. He was at least fifteen stone in weight, well built, and moved with a purposeful stride. His features were clearly recognizable and I was well acquainted with him. In fact it was not until after the sighting that I knew that I had been in the presence of a spectre.

Neither was I a dreamer. The sighting happened shortly after I had finished my two-year stint of National Service with a British infantry regiment and you know what military training means: If you see anything and it moves, you salute it. If you see it and it doesn't move, then you paint or polish it. If you see it and you can do neither of these things, then the thing does not exist.

Shortly after leaving the army, I joined the local amateur dramatic society to find my place in the community, as most of my school friends had dispersed around the country.

The society met at the Newark Technical College, a brick building constructed sometime between the two world wars in the shape of a chevron. The point of the chevron had been rounded to form an impressive entrance. To the left of this was a large multipurpose hall; one of its uses was to serve as the dramatic society's theatre. The right-hand block of the college was reserved for classrooms.

The members of the society were all friendly, but Harry, who took the male lead in most productions, was an inspiration to all newcomers, swiftly drawing them out from any initial shyness and plunging them into meaningful roles at the earliest opportunity.

Along with several other players I had developed a certain hero worship for him. On the day in question, I was rather late setting off for college, and had pedaled furiously to avoid being subject to the wrath of the other players. I duly arrived at the college and turned right at the entrance to the access point to the cycle shed. This was not the authorized way — that entailed a much longer route — but I was anxious to save time.

It did mean, however, that the side entrance, meant for pedestrians, could only be accessed by a small flight of steps. I braked sharply, lifted my cycle, and carried it up the steps.

On reaching the top I glanced toward the cycle racks and noticed Harry looking intently into one of the rear windows of the college, his hand raised to his eyes as a shield from the evening sun. I reached the cycle shed and, holding my cycle by the saddle, pushed it into a rack. As I did so I glanced again toward Harry, who turned away from the window and gave a thumbs-up sign. He smiled broadly.

I shouted to him to wait, but at that moment, my cycle, which was insecurely lodged in the rack, chose to clatter to the ground. I wasted several seconds pulling it upright and replacing it in the rack. By that time Harry had disappeared from the window, and was presumably walking along the long rear path of the building, which was obscured from view by the cycle shed. I dashed to the corner. The rear pathway was empty.

Thinking that Harry was playing a trick and he had galloped along, something that was totally inconsistent with his nature, I pressed along at top speed, reached the end of the building, dashed the few yards to the end of the chevron, and came out on the front of the college. Not a single person stood between me and the entrance hall some thirty yards away. I stopped, puzzled. There was no doorway through which he could have disappeared.

I reached the entrance and passed through into the hall. That too was completely empty. This was sinister. There should have been a rehearsal under way, and Cecil, the group leader, was a stickler for starting on time.

Suddenly the curtains parted and a face peered through. "Come along, Dennis, you are late. We're in here."

I hurried up the steps to the stage and went through the curtain. A strange sight met my eyes. It was like the Last Supper after the disciples had been told that one of them would betray Jesus. "What on earth is the matter?" I asked.

"We've just heard that Harry has had a heart attack." *That's not surprising*, I thought to myself. *Dashing round the building at that speed*. Then I realized they must have heard before I had seen Harry. "When?" I managed to gasp.

"About four hours ago. Why?"

"Oh, nothing." I could not say that I had just seen him. They would never believe me. Worse, they would think I was a sensationalist. I remembered Harry's thumbs-up sign. "You've just decided to carry on with the play, haven't you?"

"Yes. How do you know?"

"That's what Harry would have wanted. He will be at peace now."

Harry is the only ghost that I have ever seen, although sometimes when I walk along a street full of individuals frantically rushing to their destinations, I wonder, *How many of you are really there?*

Dennis Walker was born in Newark, Nottinghamshire, England, and now lives in Oakham, near Rutland Water. He is married with two grown children.

After a period of National Service in Austria and Germany, where he acquired a taste for myths, folklore, and tales of the unexplained, he studied law and is now a retired lecturer.

His writing career began with the production of revision books for law students. He then branched out into comedy writing and has had sketches produced on English, German, and Dutch television. In addition, he has contributed one-liners to radio programmes, but this is his first factual ghost story.

Ghost Walk

by Dorsey P. Leonard
Maryland, United States

I want a quiet and inconspicuous existence. The ghosts from the graves under my cottage do not. A woman died in my bedroom. I've never seen her. Her husband died on the sidewalk close to my cottage. Never seen him either. But I've seen many others who have passed, and I've seen them often. I'm the intruder, and they let me know it.

It started years ago. Everyone — including me at first — chalked it up to nightmares. Bad ones. The ones where your eyes are wide open even though you're asleep. But then I saw them in the daytime when I was awake and alert. No way were they daymares. The ghosts came to me. Their bodies were shaped by millions of rapidly moving, fuzzy, gray shadow-dots. Visual energy, faceless beam-me-ups, perfect in form and movement. They wanted me to see them and feel their presence. I did. They were there.

Nighttime became hellish.

September 10th

I awoke from a dreamless sleep for no reason. Nothing had gone bump in the night. Nothing had shaken the bed. My covers were still warm around me. The house wasn't on fire and Sooey the Siamese hadn't jumped on our mattress. But something made me waken…

There loomed a man at the door, slightly slumped and worn looking and in need of a shave. His hat wasn't quite a baseball cap, but had the same kind of brim. His shabby, unbuttoned coat had the look of a soldier's uniform. He stared in my direction, but acted as though he didn't see me. He was transparent.

I reached over and shook my husband. The ghost vanished.

"You must have dreamed it," Rick said when I told him about the man.

"No!" I insisted. "Something was here, I swear it. It disappeared when it saw me wake you up."

"You're dreaming, Hon. Come here and snuggle. Nothing will be able to get you then." Rick put his arms around me and fell back to sleep. I looked up… we were not alone.

The man was at the door again. He began to walk, a labored trudge that seemed to pain him with each step. He shuffled toward the end of my bed. I sat straight up. He kept to a straight line, passed the footboard without looking at me, then touched the outside wall. He vaporized and was gone.

I must have been dreaming. Yeah, that's it. I was dreaming.

September 16th

It was a woman in the doorway this time. She was angry. She woke me. I don't know how, but she woke me. She wore a full white dress, old-fashioned and wispy. Our wallpaper in the hall showed through her. She stared at where the man had walked through the outside wall. I screamed. She vanished. Rick woke up. Dreams again, so he said.

September 18th

Only her head this time. It perched on top of my opened bedroom door. She glared at me and her stare burned with hate. I was about to reach for Rick when the head flew off the door and came at me. I lurched to the side. She almost hit my pillow, but swooped up and landed on my headboard. I cried out. The head evaporated. Rick woke up and held me until I stopped shaking.

September 19th

My brother spent the night with us. Charlie was a single man and free to crash at anybody's house on a whim, which he did often. He preferred the couch so he could watch late-night television until he dozed off. The next morning he told me he had seen a woman in an old-looking white dress standing in the doorway. Charlie said he must have been dreaming. I said nothing.

September 20th

Sooey was acting nervous. She growled and twitched for no apparent reason. She leaped off the recliner and shot out of the living room as though the devil were at her heels. I followed her into our bedroom to find her sitting on the end of the bed. She saw something that I couldn't. Her head moved slowly from my bedroom door to the outside wall, as if watching a parade. Sooey growled again, then flew off the bed and bolted from the room.

September 21st

Lots of them this night. Soldiers, all. They were already marching past the end of my bed toward the wall when I woke up. I wasn't scared this time; it was like watching a play. None of the ghosts seemed to know I was there. Where are they going? I wondered. I watched in disbelief. I watched until my eyes grew heavy. When I fell back to sleep they were still marching.

September 22nd

This was going to be a bad day; I could feel it. The ghost shadows were around me all day, catching my eye, sometimes pressing too close. What do they want from me? Why are they faceless during daylight?

The night was the same as last, except women and children had been added to the ghostly group. I woke Rick up gently. The specters did not vanish. "See them? See them?" I whispered to Rick, pointing to our ghastly guests.

"See who?" he asked, seeing nothing.

Jesus, help me. I could still see them.

September 23rd

Exhaustion was taking its toll. What little sleep I managed was disrupted throughout the night as the uninvited woke me. In the morning the beam-me-ups followed me closely, and I could feel their presence even as I showered. They never followed when I left the house, thank God. What do they want from me? I only knew what I wanted from them — to be gone.

September 24th

Rick was asleep on his side, facing away from me. I put my hand on his arm, ready to wake him when they arrived. I didn't even bother closing my eyes. I knew they would come. They did.

My plan failed. They froze me. My hand remained on Rick's arm, but it wouldn't move. I tried to call out to him, but my mouth wouldn't open. My eyelids didn't work either. I couldn't blink. Helpless, I could only stare wide-eyed at the tattered parade of souls walking in single file past my bed and out through the wall. When they left I could move again.

I didn't bother waking Rick. He'd never believe me.

September 25th

In the shower I tried to make sense of it all. I'd heard about something called "place memory." It's supposed to be like watching a home movie of people who are dead. What you see is what they did when they were alive and in the exact place where they did it. But they're not really there. You're seeing back in time. You're seeing a memory. The place's memory.

Rick called to me, but I could barely hear him over the running water. I didn't answer him. He called my name again. Again I ignored him. The third time I turned off the shower.

"What do you want?" I hollered back at him.

Footsteps came down the hall and Rick opened the bathroom door. "You called me, Babe?" he asked.

"No, you called me three times," I said.

"No, I didn't."

September 26th

"What do you want?" Rick yelled at me from the shower. I put down the dishcloth and went to the bathroom.

"Nothing, Honey," I answered. "Why?"

"You called my name."

"No, I didn't."

So much for place memory.

September 27th

Rick flicked the shaving cream off the end of the razor, then looked up into the mirror. He was about to take another swipe.

"What the… " The razor fell from his hand and landed in the sink. He screamed for me, "Come here! Quick!"

It was easy to see he was shaken up. Rick never gets shaken up about anything. He said, "Look at that plant!"

The small hanging pot of English ivy was swinging gently back and forth on the hook. It stopped while I watched. "So what?" I asked.

"It's stopped now, but it was swinging like a son-of-a-bitch a second ago. For no reason. For no damn good reason. I saw it in the mirror; honest to God it was swinging like crazy."

"I believe you, Rick," I said, walking back to the kitchen. "I really do."

September 28th

Tonight they froze me again. Paralyzed, I was forced to watch their home movie again. But tonight "them" was different. Only two visitors, and one was a baby. The woman holding the baby appeared to be a middle-aged servant. A wide shawl covered her head and shoulders, keeping her face shadowed. She wore a long, dark skirt and a full, long-sleeved blouse. The baby was wrapped in a drab, gray blanket. The woman walked up to me and stood by the bed, but didn't seem to see me. Her head was down as if she was looking for something. She and the baby vaporized. I never saw them again after that night.

September 29th

I made the mistake of telling some friends and family about my experiences. They all thought I was nuts.

My friend, Barbara, and I had an appointment to see a Mrs. Hukill. We'd made the appointment a month before my visitations started. Mrs. Hukill was a fortune-teller. Not that I believe in fortune-tellers; I don't. It was supposed to be just for fun, a Saturday night hoot. But I wasn't laughing when it was over.

Mrs. Hukill used a regular deck of playing cards as her tools. She pulled out the queen of hearts and laid it on the table face up. She said that was me. She instructed me to shuffle the remaining cards and ask her a question as I handled the deck. I stated my question carefully. "I know someone who thinks their house is haunted. What can you tell me about it?" I finished shuffling and handed the cards back.

One by one, the fortune-teller turned the cards over, face up, and laid them around the queen of hearts. I had read somewhere that the ace of spades turned upside down is the Death Card. It was the second card she turned over.

All the cards surrounding the queen of hearts were black except one. Mrs. Hukill shook her head while she studied them. She said, "I'd tell your friend to move out of that house."

September 30th

Rick just didn't know what to make of me. He believed that I believed, but as he put it, he wasn't into any "hocus-pocus stuff." I told him everything Mrs. Hukill said. The baby is a boy (he was the one red card, the jack of diamonds). The woman holding the baby boy is not his mother, but she's seeking the mother. She's looking for the mother's tombstone. My ghosts think they're in a cemetery.

November 1st

I decided to rearrange the bedroom. Rick and I moved our bed to the opposite wall. Deep down I believed it would stop the procession; now they'd have to go around the bed if they wanted to reach the outside wall. Silly me. They simply walked through me and Rick as we lay in bed. My hands shot up defensively to push away the soldier who was walking through my stomach. My hands went through him. I scrambled out of bed, causing the procession to disappear. I was able to scream once they were gone.

This had to stop.

November 2nd

I left my bed in its new place. I'd be damned if some beam-me-up-faceless-gutless-useless-probably-not-there-anyway spooks were going to make me rearrange my life.

But this night held something different. Something more unsettling. Something more telling. No spooks or heads or babies or servants. A coffin. Just a coffin. It hung suspended in the air, halfway to the ceiling. Then I knew for sure. That coffin was part of a funeral. We were in cemeteryville. We would always be in cemeteryville.

November 4th

The groundskeeper's name was Hank Adams. He took care of the church property across the road from our cottage. There are only two tiny graveyards on the grounds, located on both sides of the church. The one on the north side is for new burials; the south side has the old graves. The historical graves. The graves of Revolutionary and Civil War soldiers.

Hank enjoyed sharing what he knew — information most people are better off not knowing. He explained, "You know those old soldier graves, the ones tourists take pictures of all the time?"

"Yes," I answered.

"Well, guess what? There ain't no bodies there. Ain't that somethin'?" Hank paused like he was waiting for my reaction. My eyebrows shot up. He had my undivided attention.

"So where are the bodies?" I already knew, but made him say the words anyway.

"Why, near about everywhere, of course. Graves probably go all the way to the highway over yonder," he stated, pointing all around, pointing toward our property.

"Why weren't the graves marked?" I asked.

"They were, for the rich. Them rich is the ones that got the stone markers. But all them poor soldiers got was wooden crosses. Didn't take no time for them to rot and break into pieces." Hank took off his cap and wiped his forehead on his sleeve. "When I was helpin' old Mr. Carr till his land — that was when he leased the north field from the church — we disked up a lot of them old tombstones. Carr told me to just pile 'em up. Down to the ravine there's still some breakin' the surface where the rain's washed the dirt from around 'em. Found a leg bone one day."

A calmness came over me; it all made sense now. "Thanks, Hank," I said. "Just one more question. How many dead are buried around here that nobody knows about?"

"Well, what with the wars and all… " Hank paused and put two fingers on his chin, "hundreds and hundreds, I'd say."

Today

I still get visitors. Seldom, but still they come. Some during the day, most at night. I'm not scared; it all adds up now. The processions really are honest-to-God funeral processions. The ghosts have to walk a straight line to move among the wooden crosses. They are too respectful to step on the graves of their dead. So they walk single file in a straight line. The line just happens to go through my bed.

I don't allow séances or fortune telling or wake-up-the-dead board games in my house. No sense in taking a chance on stirring things up again. I need my sleep.

Dorsey P. Leonard was raised on Maryland's Eastern Shore, where she resides today with her husband, Rick, and son, Derrick. Together they enjoy boating and crabbing on the scenic rivers of the Chesapeake Bay. They still live in the house where "Ghost Walk" took place, and the number of people having ghostly encounters there has grown to eight. Dorsey is the manager for a behavioral health practice, and her time at home is spent in front of the computer writing novels, short stories, and articles. She is a member of the Maryland Writers Association and the Chesapeake Writers Group.

Have *You* Had A Haunted Encounter?

If so, we'd love to hear it. Atriad Press is currently looking for true stories of supernatural experiences on various topics. A few that are coming in the near future are:

Stories of Departed Family & Friends
Real-Life Stories of Childhood Memories
Living in a Haunted House
Haunted Travel Experiences
Ghost Stories by Paranormal Investigators
Experiences of Ghost Tour Guides

And more to come!

For more upcoming titles, writer's guidelines, frequently asked questions, and more, visit our website:

www.atriadpress.com

Atriad Press
13820 Methuen Green
Dallas, TX 75240
972-671-0002